LONGY

SEAN LONG

WITH NICK APPLEYARD

LONGY

BOOZE, BRAWLS, SEX AND SCANDAL – THE AUTOBIOGRAPHY OF THE WILD MAN OF RUGBY LEAGUE

JOHN BLAKE

Published by John Blake Publishing Ltd,
3 Bramber Court, 2 Bramber Road,
London W14 9PB, England

www.johnblakepublishing.co.uk

First published in hardback in 2009
This edition published in paperback in 2010

ISBN: 978-1-84358-188-8

British Library Cataloguing-in-Publication Data:

A catalogue record for this book is available from the British Library.

Design by www.envydesign.co.uk

Printed in Great Britain by CPI Group (UK) Ltd, Croydon, CR0 4YY

5 7 9 10 8 6 4

Papers used by John Blake Publishing are natural, recyclable products
made from wood grown in sustainable forests. The manufacturing
processes conform to the environmental regulations
of the country of origin.

Every attempt has been made to contact the relevant copyright-holders,
but some were unobtainable. We would be grateful if the appropriate
people could contact us.

To my wife Claire and our three gorgeous children,
Olivia, Seini and James

CONTENTS

SEAN

I would like to thank Claire and the kids for keeping me on the straight and narrow and making me the happiest bloke alive. Cheers also to my rugby pal Glees and my oldest mates Owen and Tank for helping me remember the daft stuff I've done over the years.

NICK

Thanks to my journo colleagues Mark Harris and Julie Scott for all their help and advice. I'm indebted also to my girlfriend Emily for transcribing all the taped interviews between Sean and me; a hard task considering our crazy accents.

FOREWORD
BY JOHNNY VEGAS

What can I say about Sean that hasn't already been shouted at him from the terraces, the dugouts, the changing rooms, the boardroom, the numerous returning Hatton's coaches, the couches of all the fair weather supporters such as myself, and by that biased Yorkshire Thunderbirds villain-turned-Sky Sports commentator? Well, quite a lot actually. Some might say my interest in the man is an unhealthy one, but it is in-depth nonetheless. So, please allow me to elaborate on what I know to be the truth behind some of the myths that surround St Helens legend, Sean Long.

Sean wasn't technically 'let go' from Wigan Academy. In fact, it was carefully orchestrated by myself, as a secret 'fixer' for St Helens RLFC. The stakes were high, but it was I who met up with a nervous Maurice Lindsay in an abandoned salad bar, on Pie Street, off of Pasty Lane, in the Puff Pastry district of downtown Wigan. It was there I set in motion the wheels that were to secure for Saints one of the game's brightest young stars.

Negotiations were quite straightforward. I knew Maurice's weak spot. I stood there in my Pimblett's bikini (two meat and potato and an apple turnover), fishing rod in hand, slowly lowering jelly babies decorated in rival team kits with icing sugar into Morris's mouth, whilst all the time singing Tony Bennett's 'If I ruled the world'. I knew it was only a matter of time ... and finally he bit the head off a yellow baby Bradford Bull and agreed, with tears in his eyes, to let Sean go. I handed him back the Polaroids and bided my time. This long-secret tale has remained secret up until today and I fear it may result in Sean refusing my offer of a farewell pedalo trip along the canals and rivers that run from St Helens to Hull at the end of the season.

Still, it is revelations such as these that I hope might justify my offer to write this introduction to Sean's story. Because nobody has shaped, and subsequently followed this remarkable man's career both on and off the field, closer than I. Are we friends? I like to think so. Am I a fan? Absolutely. Was the court right in issuing that restraining order against my supposed stalking? Well, that's up to Sean and his lawyers to decide. Can I live with myself for what I did to release him from the oily clutches of Wigan? Definitely! (I always danced better without the crusty bikini).

For instance, did you know that despite his severe allergy to sterilised milk, Sean brushes his teeth with it vigorously before every match? Claiming it to be 'Nature's Viagra for your gob!', the resulting swelling provides him with a tough natural gum shield for the full eighty minutes of play. Matt Gidley, suffering from the same allergic condition, took the more extreme approach of injecting the milk directly into his gums. Unfortunately for him, the doctors say the effects are permanent.

Always looking to up his game, Sean was the first Saints player to order a back, sack 'n' crack wax at St Helens Renaissance Beauty Salon, believing his obscenely heavy growth of pubic hair was slowing him down in wet weather conditions. In his own words: 'It was like towing a wet bail of hay, I felt like I was in a tractor pull contest rather than a rugby league match.' A very jealous Scully had to make do with a highly lucrative sponsorship deal with Gillette...and lots of bits of bloody tissue stuck to his clumsily shaved groin!

It was Sean who first realised that pre-signed autographs and a staple gun was the best way of securing every single fan a memento, and an inch-wide scar to their forehead they could treasure forever. That was Longy – as innovative off the pitch as he was on it. Unfortunately, Keiron Cunningham's attempt to go one better with a nail gun forced a return to the laborious method of paper and pens for all.

But despite being the committed professional he is, Sean likes to take time out to enjoy his many hobbies. He'll often be found relaxing after matches with his beloved homing pigeons – sort of. He actually sits in St Helens Church Square with loaves of bread, luring and tagging the stray birds with ring pulls from the numerous tins of alphabetti spaghetti he consumes, in the belief that it will help broaden his limited Wigan vocabulary.

To date, none of his 'pet' pigeons have returned, but on a brighter note he no longer gets mistaken for Johnny Wellies when talking to the terrified feathered friends he is labelling.

For Sean, there have been many unfortunate injury setbacks along the way, the most notable coming after he was awarded the title Man of Steel in 2000. Believing this gifted him with superhero powers, he jumped off the roof of Chicago Rock believing he could fly to Panama Joes in time for last orders. The damage he sustained and subsequent x-rays forced the poor deluded Long to accept he was merely flesh and bone and mortal like the rest of us. The example Sean had set did not, however, stop Jamie Lyon from buying a mask and cape in 2005, and spending all his spare time throwing kittens into high trees, before attempting to rescue them. On the 97th call out of the local fire brigade and with threats of deportation from the RSPCA, Lyon was released from his contract with Saints.

I could elaborate further, trust me, but instead I'll just hope that as you sit down to read his story in his own words you can see why I have a lot of time for Sean Long. There are those who think that misconduct was his main ambition and therefore cannot enable themselves to savour the constant touches of brilliance that have brought the success we, as Saints fans, have all revelled in. I've never ceased to admire the fact that when Sean goes into a game he leaves the criticism, scepticism, derision and doubt behind him, and consistently delivers the goods. In doing so, perhaps he raised the fans expectations too high? Well, I for one did not demand Saints sign an all-round ambassador for the sport of Rugby League, just an outstanding sportsman who might let his achievements on the pitch do the talking for him, and I believe we all got far more than we bargained for in Sean Long...so for that, I thank him.

I'm just worried about what those savages from Hull are going to do to him in the showers next season. For your own safety, Sean, please, please, please – get a man's hair cut!

INTRODUCTION

When I told my mates I was writing a book, Martin 'Glees' Gleeson almost choked on his pint and said: 'Who's publishing it, fucking Ladybird?' The joke went down really well and he got a lot of laughs, the cheeky bastard.

Seriously though, I've got a few interesting tales to tell about my life on and off the rugby pitch. I've assumed the vast majority of people who've bought this book are rugby league fans, so I've made every effort not to bore you with a long-winded chronicle of my career.

To me, this book is meant to lift the lid on the crazy stuff – both on and off the field – and tell the inside story behind some of the scandalous stories I've been involved in. Of course, there might not be much left once the lawyers have been through it!

CHAPTER 1

UNSAINTLY WEEKENDS

I've been on a few jolly boys' outings with the St Helens lads over the years and there's not enough space in one book to tell you about them all. But there are two that really stand out and, you'll be pleased to learn, they're both particularly embarrassing for yours truly.

The one I still get shit for happened in July 2005. We'd just hammered Wigan 40-18 on the Friday and we were having a few drinks to celebrate. It was really sunny and warm and the forecast was the same for the weekend so, over a few pints, we decided we'd go for a bike ride on the Saturday. Mark 'Edmo' Edmondson lived in Lancaster and said: 'Come up to mine, there's loads of scenic country roads and nice pubs where we can have a couple of pints along the way.' A good, wholesome way to spend the weekend, bonding with your team-mates while getting some fresh air and exercise. Yeah, right, as if it was ever going to turn out like that!

1

There were five of us: me, Edmo, Jon 'Wilko' Wilkin, Darren 'Alby' Albert and Ady Gardner, and we all had bikes provided by Edmo's uncle, who was mad into his cycling. We got up there on the Saturday lunchtime and Edmo got the BBQ going in his garden. We had a few beers (not too many, just about six bottles each) and ate the odd burger and chicken leg before setting off on the bikes.

After a couple of miles in the sweltering sun, we stopped off at the Station pub in a village called Caton for a drink to cool down. We each had a pint and then I bought another round for the road. We were all a bit merry but it was relatively sensible until Wilko disappeared to an off licence round the corner and came back with a bottle of Jack Daniels! But no one was complaining and we all passed it round, taking a swig or two each between sups of lager. Once that bottle was empty, Wilko went and bought another one and we drank that bugger, too. It was about 3 o'clock and we'd each had half a dozen bottles of lager, two pints and about five treble JDs. We were all pissed but we weren't going to let that get in the way of our wholesome bike ride. And so we got back on the bikes and continued our tour of the country roads around Lancaster, swerving from side to side like four-year-olds on their first go without stabilisers. We cycled – or, rather, wobbled – back in the direction of Edmo's house, but took a different route in order to take in the lovely countryside. A scene that would have been an awful lot lovelier had it not been blighted by us dickheads.

We cycled for a mile or so, cheating death with every car that came by, until we came to a bridge over the

River Lune (what an appropriate name!). There was a hill up ahead and Edmo said there was a pub at the top where we could have another rest and a pint (like we needed more booze). By now, the alcohol and blazing sun had really started to take their toll and it took all my concentration to stay on two wheels. But as we crossed the bridge, I noticed Wilko get off his bike, yell 'fuck off' at it and throw the bastard in the river! He'd seen the hill coming up and decided he couldn't be arsed any more. Next minute, Alby followed suit and threw his bike over the bridge, too. I was laughing so much I almost fell off my bike, but I kept my balance and followed Edmo up the hill, leaving those two nutters behind.

I was about halfway up the hill, sweating cobs and out of breath when I heard a 'BEEP! BEEP!' coming from behind me. Before I had a chance to look round, Wilko, grinning like a maniac, came alongside me in a bloody *tractor*! 'Do you want a lift, Longy?' he asked across the farmer who was driving. 'No, you're alright, I'll see you at the top,' I said, wondering if I was seeing things. He gave me a drunken smile, stuck his thumbs up, then pointed ahead to instruct his chauffeur where to take him.

When I got to the pub – the Greyhound in Halton – about 10 minutes later, Edmo, Ady and Wilko were already there. Alby – who'd walked up the hill after ditching his bike – arrived as I brought the second round of drinks out to the beer garden where we were sat with the three remaining bikes. Then some bright spark said it would be funny to push the bikes down a steep hill round the side of the pub to see which one went furthest. We watched them tumble down and I think Edmo's bike won, but he wasn't there to enjoy his victory because he'd gone into the pub to use the toilet. Oddly enough, when he got back and saw what we'd done, he didn't seem too happy. In fact, he was fuming. He said: 'They are my uncle's bikes, my uncle's fucking bikes. Losing two's bad enough but all FIVE?' He was nearly in tears. But thankfully, he was drunk enough to listen to reason and accepted the argument that if we continued cycling in such pissed-up states, someone would end up dead.

We got taxis back to Edmo's house and all had showers, got changed and headed out into Lancaster city centre for a pub crawl. In the cab on the way there, I asked Edmo for his address in case we all got split up – a strong likelihood given the fact we were going to be mortally hammered by the end of the night. 'It's Number 4, Coronation Street,' he replied. I thought: 'Sweet, I'm not going to forget Coronation Street.'

So, we hit Lancaster at about 7 o'clock and went from pub to pub necking about eight pints to go with the shitload of booze we'd consumed in the afternoon. At around midnight, I was blotto and decided to leave the lads and go back to Edmo's house on my own to get my head down. I got a kebab, then jumped in a taxi. 'Coronation Street, please mate,' I told the driver. I'd remembered his address but if it hadn't been the title of a TV show I doubt I would have!

I sat in the passenger seat, talking gibberish to the driver, as you do, and after a few minutes we pulled into Edmo's terraced street. 'Which house is it?' asked the cabbie as he drove along. I didn't know but I was sure I'd recognise it when I saw it so I just got him to drop me off halfway down the road. I got out and thought: 'These all look the bloody same to me.' Then I remembered it was Number 4, so I walked to the end, counted two down on each side and worked out which one looked most familiar. I was in luck; the one on the left was Edmo's house. I staggered to the front door and realised I didn't have a bloody key. Jesus, I manage to find the house after all that booze and then I can't get in! I knocked on the door, just in case one of the lads had somehow arrived back before me but, predictably, there was no answer. So I sat on Edmo's doorstep, unwrapped my now-cold kebab (which I ate like a caveman), and waited. The rest of them were just as hammered as me so I didn't imagine they'd be far behind. But half an hour went by, then 45 minutes, and still no sign. Then the drunken Longy logic kicked in: 'Right, you're really tired and you need to lie down. Kick the door in and deal with it in the morning.' Sound thinking.

I tried shoulder-barging the door at first but it was doing nothing so I took a few steps back and booted it. It must have been a good kick because the bottom half of the door just caved in. It was hanging like a big cat flap so I crept through and crawled up the stairs on all fours. Once I was on the landing, I fell through the first door I came to and onto a bed. It was blissful and I was sound asleep in seconds.

At about half four, I woke up desperate for a pee and staggered to the loo. When I'd finished I went back into the bedroom and noticed I'd been asleep on the bottom of a bunk bed. 'I didn't know Edmo had kids?' I thought to myself. But then I didn't know everything about him. I went back out onto the landing and checked Edmo's bedroom and it was empty. Half past four in the morning and the lads were still going strong. Good stats!

Anyway, I took advantage of having the double bed to myself and got in. It was getting light and I lay there wondering what the boys were up to. I didn't think there was anywhere in Lancaster open that late so they must have gone to a party or maybe they'd been arrested. It would be funny if they'd all got into bother after I'd gone home early. That would make a refreshing change!

As I wondered what I'd missed out on, I looked around the room and began thinking something was up. I'd got ready in that room before we went out and things didn't look right. 'Those fucking curtains are different,' I thought. 'And I don't remember that flowery wallpaper...' Then it hit me like a sledgehammer and I sat bolt upright in bed. 'I'M IN THE WRONG FUCKING HOUSE!'

I kicked off the covers and jumped out of bed. I was bollock-naked and there was a car alarm going off in the street, which only added to my state of confusion. My hands were on my head and I was thinking: 'Shit, shit, what do I do? What if the people come home and find me starkers in their house? They'll think I'm some kind of fucking pervert!' I didn't wait for my brain to answer my questions and sprinted downstairs and into the front room. It was definitely not Edmo's place. There were photos everywhere of people who had nothing to do with him, the TV was in a different place and there wasn't an empty lager bottle to be seen. Oh, and another thing – the fucking house alarm was going off! It wasn't a car alarm outside at all. I must have activated it when I broke in, but I was so drunk I didn't realise and slept through it.

My head was going: 'No, no, no!' I had to get out of the house before the cops arrived so I frantically looked round for something to wear and found an ironing board in the kitchen with a stack of clothes on it. I grabbed the first item of clothing I could find and said to myself: 'You're naked, you're in someone else's house. Just get out of here, quick.' I ran back through the house and to the door I'd smashed in four hours earlier. I pulled on the clothes I'd grabbed from the kitchen – a pair of *black women's tights* – and scurried back out of the gap I'd booted through.

I got to my feet outside the house, wearing nothing on my top half and with my meat and two veg on clear display through the tights. 'Should I go back in and get my own clothes?' I asked myself. But I didn't have time. It was getting lighter by the minute and I had to clear off. I ran down the street, looking like I'd just escaped from an asylum for deranged trannies. As I sprinted barefoot down Coronation Street, I heard voices. It was Alby and Wilko, stood on Edmo's lawn swigging bottles of lager. 'What the fuck are you doing in a pair of tights?' Wilko asked, as though the rest of the situation was perfectly normal. I explained what had happened and they were in stitches. Alby was almost sick at one point, he was laughing that much. 'That alarm has been going off all fucking night,' Wilko chuckled.

They gave me a beer and I took them down the street

to show them what had happened. 'What am I going to do, lads?' I asked. Wilko was crouched down at the door, peering through the hole, laughing his head off. Alby was looking me up and down, shaking his head and texting people to share the funny news. While the lads were busy enjoying themselves, I crawled back through my homemade cat flap and ran upstairs to change into my clothes.

We went back to Edmo's and I said: 'Right, I'm phoning the police. I need to come clean before they come to me.' The cops had my fingerprints on file from an incident I'd been involved with when I was 18, so I was bang to rights. And even if they didn't catch up with me, I felt well guilty about trashing some stranger's front door and sleeping in their beds. I told the police what had happened, that I'd thought it was my mate's house and that I felt really bad. They said they'd send someone round.

While we waited for the police to arrive, one of the lads proudly announced that he'd thought of a new nickname for me: 'Goldilocks'. It went down a storm. A patrol car arrived within a few minutes and two coppers – both in their forties – came into Edmo's front room. 'Okay, what's the story then?' one of them asked. I told them exactly what happened, from the kebab and the taxi, to kicking the door in and falling asleep naked. At first I thought I was going to get done but with each step of the story, the coppers just laughed harder. They were both rugby fans and they knew who I was. It was obvious my story was true and I offered to pay for any damage.

The officers said not to worry about it and to just be

thankful that the owners of the house were away. If I'd broken in, stripped naked, then hopped into bed with some woman it would be a different story altogether! They'd checked with the neighbours and discovered the people who owned the house were on holiday. The police also said they'd get the doorway boarded up and would let the residents know what had happened and that it was an accident. They were really good guys, those cops. As they left, I said: 'Tell them my address and phone number and as soon as they get back I'll sort it all out, I'll pay for everything.'

It was well after 5am by the time they'd gone and it was daylight outside so we decided we might as well stay up and drink beer. But after about 20 minutes, there was another knock on the door. 'Here we go,' I thought. 'They've come back from their holiday and it's going to kick off.' I looked out of the window and it was another Panda car outside. I went to the door and there were two more policemen stood there. 'Hiya Sean, sorry to bother you,' one of them said with a smile. 'We just wanted to check it was true.' Apparently, my drunken incident was buzz of every walkie-talkie in Lancaster and the coppers all thought it was hilarious.

We stayed at Edmo's for a few more hours, watching rugby DVDs and having a bit of banter, and then we all made our way home. When I got in, I told my wife Claire what had happened and she just shrugged her shoulders and said: 'I wonder if you'll ever return from a weekend away with the lads and just say you've had a normal time?'

A few days later, the people who lived in the house rang me and I apologised for trashing their front door.

They said they'd had the shock of their lives when they got home and saw the boards and the police tape. But the police had left a contact number and explained what had gone on and the owners of the house actually thought it was really funny. They got all the damage priced up and it came to £1,500 – a lot of money for a door! I think they ended up getting a new front door and new windows to boot! But who was I to argue? I'd broken into their house and slept naked in their beds. It turned out they were an older couple and the bunk beds were for their grandkids. They became quite pally with Edmo at Number 4 and they still talk about it now. I think the night a drunken rugby player lost the plot in their house is their claim to fame!

A few years earlier, in 2000, I went to Blackpool with fellow Saints Scott Barrow and Paul 'Wello' Wellens and my good mate Tank, who I knew from school. The team were playing Castleford that Saturday but I was injured and I'd been given the weekend off. Wello was crocked, too, and Scott was just a nipper back then and hadn't been picked to play.

We got the train from Wigan on Saturday morning and were having our first pint by midday. We went round all the usual sticky-carpeted boozers like the Merrie England Bar and the Tower Lounge and spent the afternoon power drinking and chatting up girls. It was the middle of summer, the place was full of hen and stag parties, and it was buzzing. We had about a dozen pints each by teatime and then staggered back to our B&B to get changed out of our shorts and T-shirts.

We were back on the sauce by seven o'clock after a swanky meal of pie, chips and gravy at a greasy spoon café. We found a nice bar, full of girls, just off the promenade and we spent the night there. We got talking to a gang of girls from Chester who were out for their mate's birthday and I ended up chatting to a particularly fit one called Jasmine. She looked like Meg Ryan in *When Harry Met Sally* and she was gorgeous (though, I must say, not as nice as my future wife Claire!). It was all going brilliantly; she was laughing at my jokes, both of her brothers were rugby league fans (she texted one of them and he'd heard of me!) and I knew I was in there. I'd had about five pints since our teatime break but I wasn't that pissed. I was nursing my drink, conscious that I could slip back into drunkenness at any time, so when she said she was going to the bar, I passed and said I'd nip to the loo and see her back at the same spot.

I'd been dying for a pee for ages but didn't want to release my grip on the girl. I was taking a big enough risk letting her go to the bar when the place was full of blokes on heat. I went to use the toilet but the pub was heaving so I nipped outside to relieve myself in an alleyway. At least that way I could be sure of being back before her and she wouldn't be left standing on her own surrounded by the pack of wolves.

When I was deciding what to put in this book, I wasn't sure whether to include what happened next because it's a bit unsavoury. But it's quite funny at the same time, so I thought 'fuck it'.

Anyway, I walked outside and bumped into Tank, who'd also decided that getting to the toilet was too much like hard work when you've got the great outdoors to urinate in. So, there I was, wearing my white linen

11

summer trousers (without undies) and merrily peeing away against a wall and chatting to my mate when the unthinkable happened – *I shat myself*! It had never happened to me before and it never has since but there I was, within a whisker of pulling the hottest babe in Blackpool, and I'd done a poo in my trousers. Perhaps I was pushing too hard to finish my pee so I could get back to Jasmine. Or maybe it was just my body telling me I'd had close to 20 pints that day and it wasn't too happy. Either way, I was stood outside a busy pub, outside of which dozens of people were stood drinking, and I had a turd lodged halfway down my left leg. What a bloody nightmare!

I looked at Tank, thought about telling him what had happened, but realised that if I did he'd have my life. So I just ran away! My plan was to run to the beach, release the turd from my trousers, wash myself and my trousers in the sea, and then run back. No one would have to be any the wiser – least of all Jasmine. If anyone asked why my trousers had a wet patch, I'd say someone spilt a drink over me. Anyway, they'd soon dry out on a hot summer's night.

And so I bolted. I later heard that after I sped off, Tank said to Scott: 'Longy's run off to meet that bird, the wanker.' It's an unwritten rule that when you're away with the lads you don't disappear on them for a woman and if Tank was right, I'd have deserved to get it in the neck. But he couldn't have been more wrong. I was on the beach inside of two minutes and all I could think was, 'I've got to get rid of this turd.' It was pitch black and I could only just make out the sea by the reflection of the promenade lights on the water. I was stood in the sea, with the water just covering my sandals, and I'd just started undoing my trousers when this huge wave hit me and knocked me flying. I was a lot drunker than I thought and my legs were like jelly. The sea dragged me out and I began to panic big-style. I swallowed a load of water and I was out of breath. I managed to get to my feet but I was soaked through and weighed down by my clothes and when the next wave came at me, I was powerless to resist it. I was back down again, thrown around by the water. My sandals were both gone and one second I was above the water, seeing flashes of the promenade lights through blurred vision, and the next I was pushed back down to the sea bed and dragged along the sand. I really thought I was a goner. I fought for my life for about five minutes before eventually swimming free. I crawled back onto the beach, coughing up sea water. I got to my feet and thought: 'What the fuck? I nearly killed myself over a turd!'

I was soaking wet, my sandals were washed out to sea and I was exhausted. My mission now was to get back to the digs and get my head down. I ran to the B&B, raising a few laughs and the odd concerned face from passers-by along the way. It was after midnight and the B&B was locked up for the night. My key – as well as my wallet and my phone – were lost during my battle with the sea. And so I banged on the door. I saw a light come on upstairs and thought to myself: 'What's the landlord going to make of me, dripping wet and covered with sand?'

When he opened the door, he looked me up and down and said: 'Good God, son, what the hell's happened to you?' There I was, barefoot, grazed, gasping for breath and looking like a sand monster from a 1950s B-movie. I couldn't tell him that I'd shat myself and then nearly drowned while trying to free the turd. So, in true Longy style, I said the first thing that came into my head: 'I've been mugged'. He was really sympathetic and said: 'You poor sod. Come inside, son, and let's get you out of those wet clothes.' He took me into the kitchen and I took off my shirt and my trousers. I had no undies on so I was bollock-naked (there's a theme going on here). When I passed him my clothes, he suddenly lurched his head backwards and gagged. 'There's shit everywhere!' he said, a look of disgust on his face. I'd not noticed. It must have spread all over me as I was being tossed around by the waves. My quick thinking kicked in again: 'Oh, yeah, the muggers shit on me as well.' The mugging tale had won me sympathy, but now I'd taken it too far. 'You lying bastard,' he snapped. 'I don't know what you've been doing and I don't want to know.' He said he'd wash my clothes for me and then he sent me up to the room I was sharing with the lads. The others weren't back yet and I just fell onto the first bed I came to and passed out.

A few hours later, the lads returned and Tank woke me up. 'Where did you fuck off to?' he asked. 'You sloped off with that bird, didn't you?' The look of anger on his face soon turned to one of ecstasy as I began recounting the whole sorry story. I have never seen Tank laugh so hard in all my life. 'I could have died, you know, Tank,' I said. That only made him laugh harder.

The next morning, we all woke up with shocking hangovers. But funnily enough, I wasn't as bad as the rest of them because I'd stopped drinking hours earlier, though I was aching like I'd done a couple of rounds with a professional boxer. We all decided that we needed a hair of the dog and so we left the B&B – I didn't have the nerve to find the landlord and ask for my clothes – and walked down to the Merrie England Bar for a few pints before getting the train home. Scott was really rough and he just sat with his head in his hands. He couldn't bring himself to even sip a beer. The rest of us had a couple of pints and had a laugh about my unfortunate incident the night before.

Things took a turn for the good when a gang of about 20 girls came into the pub and sat with us. They were all from St Helens so they knew who we were. 'What's up with him?' asked one of them, pointing towards Scott. I said: 'Ah, well, it's quite a funny story, actually...' And so, while Scott sat with his head in his hands, half-sleeping and fighting the urge to vomit, I told all the girls how he had shat himself and how he nearly drowned afterwards as he tried washing himself in the sea. They were all laughing and pointing at him, going, 'Uurgh, you're disgusting!' and jokingly wafting their hands in front of their noses. Poor Scott didn't even have the energy to protest. All he could do was mumble, 'It were him', and point at me but I just went, 'You just sleep it off, Scott. It could have happened to anyone.'

Of course, it couldn't have happened to anyone. Shit like that (no pun intended) only seems to happen to numpties like me.

CHAPTER 2

POACHING, SKIVING AND SMOKING – AGED 5!

I came into this world on September 24, 1976, and my mum and dad tell me I was a fast developer. I was walking at 10 months and talking (not coherently but hey, that's not changed) a few months after that. My mum says I no longer needed nappies by my second birthday. She hasn't seen me after 15 pints!

We had no money when I was really young. My little brother Karl was born when I was four and Mum looked after us two while Dad did his best to find work. There wasn't much work around so Dad was in and out of jobs for years – mostly out, unfortunately. But my folks never let a shortage of brass keep us Longs from having food on the table, even if the way Dad procured it was not exactly legal.

I was about four when I first saw Dad get ready to go poaching in his camouflage gear. I was dressed for bed and watching telly when he came into the front room and sat next to me on the couch to lace up his boots. I remember thinking that he must be in the Army. I asked where he was going and Mum said he was 'off to get some rabbits and spuds from the fields' and I pleaded to go with him. He went out most nights, usually poaching rabbits, pheasants, hares and wood pigeons and from then on, I pestered every time to go with him. But he couldn't be arsed with a little boy getting under his feet, wanting a carry half the time, especially when he might have to do a runner at any moment from a trigger-happy farmer.

But eventually my pester power proved stronger than my dad's resolve and after about a year he gave in and let me go with him on a potato raid. I remember that first night vividly. He gave me a tiny little sack and he had a big bloody thing and we drove out to the countryside, me in the passenger seat of his brown Capri. I was five years old, up way after my bedtime, and as excited as you get on Christmas Eve. We went just outside of town, a few miles from our terraced house in Wigan, to where all the farms were. We parked up a country lane and when we got out of the car it was pitch black and pouring with rain. Good job I had my Spiderman wellies on!

I was quite scared at first but once my eyes adjusted to the dark I was fine. Dad picked me up and we squeezed through some bushes and onto the farmer's field. We had to climb a little hill, then Dad quickly went to work filling his sack with spuds and I did the same. We were only there for about five minutes when Dad said we had to scarper. He started walking back to the gap in the bushes and swung his sack over his shoulder. I copied him and the weight of my sack sent me flying backwards and I slid down the hill through the mud, getting caked from head to toe. I couldn't get up so I shouted for Dad and he turned round, laughed his head off and said, 'Come on, let's get this lot in the car before someone sees us.' Looking back, I was like the kid out of the Roald Dahl story *Danny, Champion of the World*!

I went out with Dad loads after that, pinching food for Mum to cook for us all. And after a few months, he took me out for some proper poaching. He didn't let me use his gun when we went shooting, though. He said he didn't want me killing him, or, even worse, killing myself. I was willing to take the risk on both points but, sadly, he stood firm. Instead, I was in charge of keeping the dogs and ferrets under control until he needed them. Dad set nets at warren holes and then we sent the ferrets down to chase the rabbits out. If they escaped from the nets, the lurchers and Jack Russells went after them. People have asked me what I would have been if I hadn't been a rugby player and I say I'd have made a good poacher. When I finally hang up my rugby boots, I reckon I'll take it up as a hobby. Have you seen the price of organic meat these days?

Sometimes there would be six or seven rabbits all lying dead on the kitchen table, waiting to be gutted and skinned. I remember Mum saying to me: 'Whatever you do, don't press the rabbits' bellies otherwise they'll pee all over the floor.' Fancy saying that to a mischievous little lad! At the first opportunity I put this amazing nugget of knowledge to the test and found Mum to be true to her word. The kitchen floor was awash with rabbit pee! By the time Mum realised what I'd done I was out playing with my mates in the fields round the back of our house. And I knew I was in trouble when I heard those familiar words, 'SEAN, YOU LITTLE SHIT!' bellowing from our garden. I got a serious bollocking off Mum and a good clip off my dad. I didn't do it again.

As well as helping to catch the animals, I also plucked and skinned them. I wasn't allowed to use a sharp knife for a few years so my dad would start me off and I'd pull the skin off. My mum has a photo of me aged about five, covered in blood and grinning as I proudly hold a skinned rabbit. I wasn't squeamish about it because I'd seen my folks do it all the time and it was just normal to me. I reckon being used to all that blood from an early age helped prepare me for some of the gory injuries I've had over the years!

I was never a house kid and when I wasn't out poaching, I was always out in the fields round the back of our house building dens with my mates, playing football and pursuing my main passion, which was collecting birds' eggs. It's not very PC these days but all the local kids were into it where we lived in the early 1980s and I had a great collection that I kept in a wooden display case in my bedroom. I got a book for my fifth birthday matching birds to their eggs and I was an expert. Even now, I'd happily challenge Bill Oddie to a match-the-egg-to-the-bird contest! I had common ones like blackbirds, coots, sparrows and dunnocks. Then one day I found a meadow pipit's nest in a hole in the ground with four eggs inside. I took two – one for my collection and one to swap with my mates. We never took all the eggs from a nest; even as kids we knew that would be wrong. I swapped a meadow pipit egg for a kestrel one and I had the best collection around. It was my pride and joy and I'd spend ages at bedtime, counting the eggs and rearranging them.

We lived in an area of Wigan called Worsley Mesnes. At the time, it was well rough and full of dodgy people. One bedtime when I was about five or six, I was lining my birds' eggs up along my windowsill when I saw this bloke – who I think was care in the community – run out from his flat, across the area of grass where we played football, and throw a brick through the front window of a house. Two lads lived there, they must have been about 18, and they sprinted out and battered the living daylights out of him. It's not a nice thing for a little lad to see from his bedroom window, and Mum said we had to get out of the area.

We lived in a two-up two-down end-terrace house and there was a shop over the road where all the older lads used to hang out. When I was five – I remember because I had just started school – I began going down to the shop to hang out with them. I was a little shit, always answering back, swearing and getting into scrapes. I suppose I was a blue version of Bart Simpson. Before my sixth birthday I was picking fag butts up off the pavement and smoking them. Three foot tall and smoking! I'd seen my parents smoke and the big lads were doing it, so I thought 'Why can't I?' But one day I was minding my own business, puffing away on a fag while kicking my football against a wall when I felt a grip on my shoulder. It was Mum. I threw the ciggie on the floor and tried to act all innocent, hoping against hope that she hadn't seen. Oh, the optimism of youth! I

21

was caught red-handed and she went MAD! But that telling-off was a walk in the park compared to the bollocking I got off Dad when I got home. My fag habit ended that day.

At around that time, something happened to me that sent my world crashing around my ears. I got home from school one day to find that my little brother had taken it upon himself to smash all my birds' eggs. I'd put them in my wardrobe for safe-keeping but the little shit – he was only three – found them and clearly didn't realise how important they were to me. When I saw my prized collection destroyed, I was inconsolable. Crying, I ran downstairs and told Mum what had happened. There was only one person who could have done it and I shouted at our Karl and made a dash for him. But Mum stopped me and explained that he was only small and he didn't know what he was doing. Him chanting, 'Eggs smashed, eggs smashed' didn't help, but I calmed down. I vowed there and then that when he was big enough I would give him a good hiding. Unfortunately, by the time I got round to it, Karl was a lot bigger than me and quite a hard bugger. But if you're reading this, our Karl, I'm still waiting for my moment!

Every morning I walked to school, St Jude's Primary, on my own and I used to pass some of the older junior lads who were loitering outside the shop, bunking off. One day, aged six and in my second year at infants, I thought, 'sod it, I'm not going to school either' and went with them to watch telly at one of their houses. But I found it boring, so I went to the junior school to meet my friends at dinnertime. I sat on the grass outside the Junior One classroom and waited for them. Some of my mates saw me through the window and pointed and waved at me. Then the teacher opened the window and pointed down the road to the Infants and said: 'You're down there. Get to your own class.' But I had my brilliant excuse – the kind of lie that was to blight my mischievous childhood – ready. I said: 'It's ok, my mum has given me the day off.' She asked why and I gave the clever answer: 'I'm looking after my little brother.' She then pointed out that I was alone, and my mates all had a good laugh. I just walked off and went home, knowing that my folks would find out about it. I got in at three o'clock, 45 minutes earlier than usual, and Mum asked why I was home so soon. Knowing the inevitable, I came clean and got my usual two-pronged bollocking: a good shouting-at off Mum, followed by a crack off my dad when he got in. They were pissed off and looking back I don't blame them – I was an ex-smoker and I was skiving off school. And I was only six!

According to my folks, I was a little shit pretty much from the day I was able to crawl. My cousin Paul, who's about five months younger than me, used to go through hell when we played together as little kids. From the stories my mum tells me I was like Chucky off *Child's Play*, hitting Paul and any other kids with anything from rusks to plastic hammers that squeaked on contact.

I continued being a little sod and was always in trouble at school, but it wasn't till Junior One that I got my first real bollocking (outside the family home, that is!). The teacher was reading a story and she said the name 'Aunt Fanny'. I started laughing 'cause I knew what a fanny was, even though I was only seven. I looked over to my mate Jason Callaghan, who was laughing his head off as well. I had my head in my hands, my shoulders bouncing up and down and the teacher stopped reading from the book. I could sense she was looking at me but I didn't dare look up. I knew I was going to get told off, but I couldn't stop laughing. After all, the teacher had said the word 'fanny'! When she yelled 'SEAN!' I looked up, tears of laughter running down my face, and she said: 'Go to the headmaster's office, NOW!' She pointed at Jason and ordered him to go with me.

We were marched out of the classroom and through the school to the Head, an old wizard-like man called Mr Lynch – an appropriate name for a guy who loved to punish. The teacher explained what terrible crime we'd committed and left us in the room with him. I will never forget that old git because he fucking caned me! Just for finding the word 'fanny' funny. I was a cocky kid with a smart answer for everything, but when I saw him take the cane off his bookshelf I don't think I could have spoken a single word for the life of me. He told me to hold my right hand out and when I did, I took a deep breath and concentrated on not letting it shake. I didn't want him to know how scared I was. He was enjoying it enough already.

He lifted his hand in the air and brought the cane down with huge force, right on the ends of my fingers. He was a good shot, I'll give him that. He only hit me once but the pain was incredible. Jason got his caning after me, while I stood next to him, fighting back tears. I had to look away when he got his. I knew what was coming. We went back to the classroom holding our throbbing fingers and blubbing to ourselves. When we got in, we were sent to the back of the class but I got the impression the teacher felt a bit bad that we'd been caned. I think she thought we'd just get shouted at.

As well as the pain, I vividly remember how wronged I felt for getting caned for such a little thing. I didn't deserve such harsh punishment. I wasn't a bad lad; I didn't hit people or bully them. I was just a bit daft and cheeky. Just after that, caning in schools was banned. I think Jason and I were the last kids in St Jude's Primary to get the cane. Can't say I learnt my lesson, though. 'Fanny' still makes me smile to this day!

Just weeks after being caned, I discovered the thing that ended up being the making of me – rugby. After school one day, I joined in with some of the older lads who were having a throw-about with a ball. There were only about eight of us practising, just in our school uniforms, tackling and messing about. Afterwards, I was walking home with two brothers, Lee and Barry Owen, and I asked them what they were doing that night and they said they were going to St Jude's Rugby Club for practise. They were bigging it up, saying it was 'proper rugby' where they had to pay subs and everything, like it was an exclusive club. I was impressed. 'Can I come, can I come?' I asked, and they invited me down.

I went home and had my tea, packed my PE kit, and walked the mile-and-a-half to the club for training at six o'clock. I didn't tell my mum and dad where I was going; they just thought I was playing out. When I got there all the lads were 10 or 11 years old; they were loads bigger than me. Lee and Barry introduced me and said I wanted to play and there were a few shrugged shoulders but they let me join in. I didn't even have the 30p subs but they said I could pay it next time. I had a great time, running round after the ball like a blue-arsed fly and tackling the big lads. I had caught the rugby bug.

When I got in that night I told Mum and Dad where I'd been and they were made up. They just looked at each other and smiled. My dad was really into rugby; he played loads as a kid and watched it all the time on the telly. From that day on my dad did all he could to fuel my love of the game. He took me to watch Wigan play, though he never paid for me. When we got to the window at Central Park, he told me to duck down and he'd pay for himself. I'd scuttle along crouched down for a few feet and when we got to the turnstiles he'd say, 'I'm just going to lift this little lad over, alreet?' and no one gave a shit. All the dads did that back then. They wouldn't get away with it now at the JJB where it's all computerised and your ticket has a bloody barcode on it.

Anyway, I became rugby-mad and I took my first ball – that my nan and granddad bought for me – everywhere I went. Corporation Park, where St Jude's trained and played, was a shithole, though. There were two pitches that were always waterlogged and muddy. Along one side were allotments and a pig farm and I'm sure that half the time we were diving around in pig shit that the rain had washed onto the field. But I was seven and being covered from head to foot in mud or pig poo wasn't a problem. It was a good job swine flu wasn't around at the time or I'm sure the place would have been a no-go zone!

I had a good idea that where we lived wasn't very nice, but what really sealed it for me was the day I was shot in the back, still aged only seven, by some older neighbourhood lads. Back then, a lot of the older boys had air rifles and they used to bully the little kids into letting them take a shot at you. One summer's night I was on my way home from playing hide-and-seek in the fields with my mates when three brothers, who lived a few streets down from me, came over. They were older than me, probably in their early teens, and they made me stand still and lift my T-shirt up so they could shoot me. It was only an air rifle so it wouldn't hurt, they assured me. Looking back it sounds really stupid, but back then, you did what the big lads asked. I suppose it was a rite of passage thing in an area where big kids were shitty to little kids. The same probably happened to them when they were small. We were behind a social club near my house and I lifted my T-shirt up and closed my eyes. They lied – it did hurt, it hurt me like hell. But I didn't let it show and I held it in and ran home, being careful not to cry until I was round the corner, out of sight. When I got in the house, my eyes were streaming but when Mum asked me what was wrong, I said 'nothing', and ran up to my room. I remember looking in the mirror at the big bruise on my back and hating those lads. That was the kind of place it was – full of fucking scumbags. If those three fancy their chances now, they know where I am.

But away from the nasty sods who lived near me, down at St Jude's I was always assured of a warm welcome and the feeling of togetherness you can only get by being part of a team. Because I was younger – a full four years younger – than the rest of the Under-11s squad I rarely got a game in those early days. I was there to make up the numbers. But I didn't care; I just loved being part of the squad.

Oddly, one of my first games for the club was for the Under-12s. They were short one day and asked the Under-11s coach if they could borrow a sub and he said: 'Go on Sean, you can play.' The game started and I was on the sidelines as the team's one and only replacement. Looking back it was madness, a skinny lad of nine facing up to 12-year-olds. Some of them looked like fully-grown men to me. But that didn't faze me and I was itching to have a go. My prayers were answered when, with about 10 minutes to go, the game was slowing and I was released onto an unsuspecting bunch of big lads.

They put me on the wing, where they probably figured I couldn't get into too much trouble. But they didn't allow for my kamikaze instincts. Most of the play was going down the opposite flank to where I was positioned and, looking back that was probably why they put me there. But I was so keen to get involved I ran right across the pitch to tackle and then all the way back to where I was supposed to be playing. I remember seeing Dad on the touchline shaking his head in disbelief, clearly thinking 'what the fuck is he doing?' But I knew he was proud as punch to see me on the park competing with kids who were literally, in some cases, twice my size.

Shortly after that, I came home with a medal. I was with the Under-11s this time and we were playing Black Brook Rugby Club in St Helens. Again I was on the bench, stood by the touchline, hoping they'd give me 10 minutes on the wing or whatever. I didn't get a game but after the final whistle, I was walking off the pitch when a ball came hurtling over in the direction of a woman pushing a pram. It was headed right for her baby and so I quickly dived and knocked the ball off course. The woman was really thankful. Next minute the coach came up to me and said, 'Well done son, you did great there' and he gave me a gold medal with the club's name on it, hanging by a ribbon. I was only seven or eight and I was buzzing. I put it round my neck and raced home, thinking how proud Dad would be. I bolted into the house, grinning from ear to ear and brandishing my first ever rugby medal. Dad went: 'Bloody hell, where have you got that from?' I replied: 'Well, they brought me on for the second half and I scored three tries and got man of the match.' He was chuffed to bits and jumped out of his chair to admire my prize. 'Three tries!' he exclaimed, 'That's bloody great, son. Did you really score three tries?' I could sense that the lie was going to come back and bite me on the arse but it was too late now. 'Yeah,' I said, as if trying not to be big-headed, like it was no big deal.

The following Sunday, Dad came along to the game and my fib was found out big-style. We were stood on the touchline, watching my Under-11 team-mates, and Dad boasted to one of the other parents stood next to us: 'Did you see our Sean last week? He scored three tries, you know.' The bloke replied: 'He didn't get a game, mate.' I witnessed the exchange and it felt like it was in slow-motion. I was thinking: 'Christ, I'm for it now.' My Dad looked down at me and I expected a right clip. But despite the embarrassment he obviously felt, I think he was a bit amused by it and he muttered those three all-too-familiar words: 'You little shit.'

During those first couple of years I didn't make a full-time member of the team, just the occasional run-out when they were short or the odd 10 or 15 minutes at the end of a game to shut me up. But when I was nine I was picked to play full back for the Under-11s. I didn't have any ball skills but I was bloody good at tackling. Time and again the big lads would make breaks through the middle and, smack, I'd take them down. I don't think there's a rugby player who wouldn't agree there's nothing better than taking down a bigger bloke than you and hearing him thud to the ground. In those age group games there were always some lads who had put on a growth spurt and were twice as wide and twice as tall as their mates. They would find it easy to make the breaks but I'd find it even easier, as the last line of defence, to put them down. I'm not talking about big hits; I was too small for that. These were textbook tackles – I'd grab them round the thighs and slide down to their ankles. With a little fucker like me wrapped round their legs it was impossible to run anywhere!

That ability to tackle got me noticed. My dad always cut out and kept any mentions I got in the local paper. One early report of a defeat for St Jude's Under-11s reads: 'St Jude's Under-11s lost 28-0 to Woolston. Man of the match yet again was Sean Long with some try-saving tackles'. Defensive play has always been as big a part of the game as attack – that's why so many rugby league coaches are now coaching union sides – and if you make your tackles then it won't be long before you make an impression. And that's how I came to be picked to play full-back for the Lancashire Under-11s side during the 1985/86 season. At just nine years old I was the youngest player ever to pull on a Lancashire shirt. Rugby league legend-to-be Andy Farrell was in that same team.

Once I was playing Under-11s rugby with lads my own age, I came into my own and they moved me to stand-off. When I was 10, my dad started coaching at St Jude's and he remained my coach till I was 16. Having your dad as coach is good and bad. The problem with being coached by your old man is that if, like me, you mess around in training, throwing mud around and taking the piss, you get bollocked at training AND at home. The other lads used to laugh when my dad told me off because I always got it in the neck more than them. When other players got sidelined for being daft, I was sent to the family car where I'd have to sit until Dad whistled for me to come out.

But the worst thing for me was that no matter how badly the other lads behaved in training, they could tell their dads when they got home that they'd trained really hard. When Dad and me got home and Mum asked how training went, I'd say 'great' and Dad would say, 'No it didn't, he was a little shit.' Then I'd get done all over again while we were having our tea. My dad would calm down on the drive home, but by asking how it had gone, Mum would accidentally set him off again. It wasn't easy being me sometimes!

But even back then, I knew it was doing me good, that I needed more discipline than many of the other lads. Dad was a good coach and he was extra strict with me because I needed it. He also saw the potential in me. If I was allowed to fool around all the time, I wouldn't improve quickly enough to make it in the game.

As well as my new-found love of rugby, things took another turn for the good when my mum's Uncle Ned and Auntie Amelia said they had a caravan that was stood empty at their farm in New Springs, just outside of Wigan. It was a much nicer area, away from kids with guns and the tight bastards who'd say hello to you then rob your house the minute your back was turned. So we packed up and moved in. To make things even better for us Longs, my mum found work at a local bakery and Dad got a job as a flagger in Bolton. We finally had a bit of money coming in and we didn't need to go poaching any more. I went to a different school, called The Holy Family, and I calmed down a bit. I was still a rum 'un but I didn't bunk off.

The caravan was a great place to be for a young lad and me and Karl loved every minute of the 18 months we were there. Mum and Dad had the main – and only – bedroom and us kids slept in the front. In the morning, me and Karl had to fold our beds up and put the table up for breakfast – like you do on holiday. To us, it was one big holiday. We used to go with Uncle Ned to get all the eggs in from the chickens and it was great because they nested in the old tractors that were lying about the farm so we had to climb around them and get in the nooks and crannies to get the eggs. I loved doing that job. But one farm task I hated was mucking the pigs out. I only did it a few times and it was bloody hard work, though we had fun getting chases off the pigs. Me and Karl would jump into the pen and flash our bare arses at them and they went mental, running after us, trying to hump us. We'd run out of the way then dive back in and get another chase. It was a brilliant buzz and great rugby training! In the time we were at the caravan, our folks saved up a deposit on a house and they bought a place in Whelley, about a mile and a half away, where I lived for the rest of my childhood.

CHAPTER 3

DISCOVERING RUGBY AND GIRLS

At the age of 11, I went to St Joseph's Comprehensive school in Horwich, near Bolton. It was a Catholic school where all the kids from my Catholic primary school went, even though it was miles away. But it was a nice enough school and I had some good times there. The only problem was that when it came to sport it was 100 per cent football; they didn't play any rugby. Thankfully, I had a decent left peg on me and played on the left wing for the school football team and for the Bolton Under-13s.

But for me, football wasn't a patch on rugby and playing for St Jude's always came first. If ever a game of football clashed with rugby, football lost out. Most of my rugby mates at St Jude's went to Deanery High School in Wigan and played for the school team. It was really frustrating that I couldn't play for my school and I felt I was losing out on the extra training and match experience. My dad agreed and said it was important I represented my school in order to develop my game and further my career. A lot of the scouts were going to schools games, looking for talent, and if I was going to make it as a player, I couldn't afford not to be seen. So after two happy years at St Joseph's, I left at the beginning of the third year and went to Deanery High. It was no mean feat, getting into that school. Deanery was Protestant and I'm a Catholic. But Dad spoke to the headmaster, Mr Williams, who, fortunately, was a massive rugby fan. The school had the best rugby league team around and he wanted to keep it that way. My dad said I was the best player they'd ever have. It was a big boast but Mr Williams swallowed it and he let me in.

My dad took my rugby very seriously and he was very strict with me. A lot of my mates at that time had paper rounds or milk rounds and they always had a few quid. But Dad wouldn't let me have a job. He said getting up that early every morning would make me too tired for rugby. He was right, but at the time I thought he was a right bastard.

When I was 15, Mum and Dad split up. I'd kind of known things weren't right for ages. Dad worked long hours and then he'd be training at the gym or coaching at St Jude's. He was never at home. I felt sorry for Mum and could see them drifting apart. They started sleeping and sitting in separate rooms, which I knew wasn't right, and they were having bust-ups all the time. One afternoon, all four of us were in the house when the shit really hit the fan and we found out Mum had been having an affair. We had two phones and Mum was talking to her new bloke on one while dad was in the other room. Dad picked up the phone and heard them talking. He had no idea Mum was seeing someone else until then. Karl and me were upstairs at the time and it all kicked off in the kitchen. We could hear what they were saying and went down. Then my mum said she was going, and my dad was saying to her 'get out, get out'. Then Mum looked at Karl and me and said: 'Come on you two, you're coming with me.' I looked at her and then at my dad and said: 'No, I'm stopping here.' Mum was crying and instead of telling us, she asked this time: 'Are you coming, are you coming?' She was expecting us to go, after all everyone goes with their mum, don't they? But, much as I loved her, I said I wanted to stay where I was.

When Mum moved out, she went to live in a flat with her new guy, Tony. She was happy and I could see that. Tony's a sound bloke and they're made for each other. They're still together now. At the time, I could see my folks were better off apart but our Karl didn't take it too well. He was only 11 and it hit him really badly. He rebelled at school after that and got himself in a load of bother.

Because Dad was working long hours for the flagging firm, I had to help our Karl out a lot. I suppose I became a kind of surrogate dad to him. All the teachers at school knew what had gone on and they would come to me and ask me to help Karl. He did daft things that were obviously going to get him into trouble; I don't know whether they were cries for help or what. At the Deanery they had this thing where you had to back your textbooks to protect the covers. I was called into the Head's office one day where he had Karl and one of his books that he'd backed with pages from a porno magazine. He asked me what I thought and I took one look at our Karl and said: 'Nice tits.' Needless to say it didn't go down well, but me and my bro had a laugh after our mutual bollocking.

We used to sneakily nip up and see Mum and it was hard at the time. But even back then, I knew it was for the best. My dad is a bit of a crazy character and he dated a few girls, but he found it hard. I felt sorry for him because he'd get up at six in the morning and work a long shift while still keeping on top of all the housekeeping stuff. But it had its good points. Because Dad was out of the house hours before I had to go to school, it was pretty much up to me whether or not I bothered going. I'd wake up and think 'fuck Maths' or 'fuck Science' and I'd just roll over and go back to sleep. I'd pick and choose whether to go to school and my dad didn't know. The fact was, I knew rugby was going to be my life and so did Dad. I was going to play professionally and that was that.

Me and my best mate Richard Owen – who everyone calls by his surname – never did our homework. It was sort of an unwritten rule we had between us that neither of us did it so that when we got done off the teacher, we got done together. After all, a bollocking shared is a bollocking halved. I remember one time in fourth year Geography we were meant to hand in a quiz sheet we'd been given. I think I'd made a paper aeroplane with mine on the way home from school the week before. As far as I was concerned, I was playing rugby most nights so didn't have time for school stuff. And even if I did (which, to be honest, I did) knowing about mountains and glaciers and shit like that was not going to make me a better player.

Anyway, we all went into the lesson, as usual, a few minutes before the teacher got there, and I said to Owen: 'Have you done your homework?' It was a rhetorical question because I knew he was just going to say no. But the bloody Judas started laughing and waving his sheet and said he'd copied the answers off someone at lunchtime! I couldn't believe it and I was fuming at the sly bastard. We got to our desks and he was teasing me with it from across the class. So, while everyone else was getting their books and stuff out of their bags, I got up, snatched it off him and started eating it. He was grabbing at me, trying to get it out of my mouth when the teacher, Mr Parkinson, came into the room. He saw me scrapping with Owen and he shouted: 'What's that? What's that in your mouth, Long?' I started laughing, which with my mouth full just meant snorting through my nose, and spat it out onto the floor. Then Owen, pretending to be all conscientious and gutted that someone was eating the work he'd spent ages on, said: 'He's eaten my homework, Sir.' Mr Parkinson went mental. He stormed over and dragged me off my seat while Owen was looking on, laughing to himself. But Mr Parkinson grabbed him as well, took us both outside and gave us the biggest bollocking ever. Other teachers came out of their classes to see what was going on, it was that bad. But when they saw it was us two getting it, they all just shrugged as if to say 'fair enough' and went back to their classes. I had to pay one of my regular visits to the Head's office that day. I was sent to see him so often that he recognised my knock.

The school toilets are not just for pissing in – they are for pissing about in. There were about five of us in the toilets one dinnertime and one of the lads started flicking water. It soon escalated to a full-on water fight and before we knew it we were all drenched and the place was flooded. The caretaker heard the commotion and came storming in. She was called Mrs Tickle, but don't let the funny name fool you into thinking she was the happy type. She was a grouchy old thing and she dragged us out of the toilets, lined us up in the corridor and railroaded us. Nobody really took her seriously because she didn't have any authority, but that didn't stop her acting like she was in the Gestapo.

She got to the first lad, Chris Holden, and said: 'Right, you're all going to see the headmaster, I want your name.' So Chris, just being cheeky, went: 'Mr Holden.' Mrs Tickle barked: 'It is not Mr Holden, it is *Master* Holden.' And so, she worked her way along the line and everyone followed suit: 'Master Owen', 'Master Long' etc. She got to Danny Stapleton (a sharp-witted lad) at the end and asked: 'And what's your name?' Quick as a flash he answered: 'Mr Bates'. So, right on cue, Mrs Tickle said: 'It is not Mr Bates, it is *Master Bates*.' We were still laughing when we arrived at the Head's office.

'What are you lot here for?' asked Mr Williams. He turned to me and said: 'I should change the name on that door to Long!' Mrs Tickle was stood next to us, her arms folded and her face looking cross. No one dared speak at first, for fear of bursting out laughing. Finally, Owen told the story and when he ended it with: 'And then Mrs Tickle said "it's not Mr Bates, it's Master

Bates..."' we all erupted into howls of laughter. You could see the Head was dying to laugh; I reckon if Mrs Tickle hadn't have been there, he'd have wet himself.

As you might have gathered, I didn't take my school career at all seriously. I knew I was going to be a rugby player and that's all that mattered; I had a one-track mind. My attitude was daft really because if it went tits up I'd have been knackered. People knew I had a talent but there's lots of lads like me with ability who don't make it, either through injury or just by not developing as expected. I should have hedged my bets by studying a bit but, for me, going to school was about seeing my mates and chatting up girls.

Speaking of girls, one bonus of having a dad who was always working or training and a mum who lived elsewhere was being able to bring lasses home without getting any earache. But despite having our house at my disposal for carnal activities, I ended up losing my virginity at my best mate Owen's gaff.

We were all 15 and it was the Deanery Christmas party at a club in Wigan called Maxine's. The school had hired the place for the night, so obviously there was no booze behind the bar. Me, Owen and the two girls we were seeing had all been building up to the Christmas do as the night we'd all do it. Owen and me were both prepped up and had two johnnies each in our wallets, ready for some serious action. I'd seen loads of pornos so was quietly confident I would perform well. After the party, we went back to Owen's and it was straight down to business. Owen went: 'Right, Longy, I'm in my room and you're in my brother's room.' And so I went up the stairs with Cathy, exuding the air of a lad who was ready to give her the jump of her life. It was too late to tell Owen – who already had a couple of notches on his bedpost – that I was getting nervous. We did the deed on Owen's brother's single bed and it was a right let down. I realised that being good at sex on my own didn't necessarily mean I'd be good when someone else was involved! I didn't know what to expect and half-thought it was going to be some magical thing that would make me feel somehow different afterwards, like I'd evolved. It didn't help that the condom split at one point, meaning my head was in the shed for ages afterwards, wondering if I'd have a sprog to contend with nine months down the line.

As I was having my awkward fumble with Cathy, Owen was in the room next door and it sounded like there was a porn shoot going on in there. He was the most well-endowed lad in our school and clearly knew what to do with his gift. Screams of 'YES! YES!' and the sound of bedsprings moving to Owen's experienced rhythm were enough to put anyone off – let alone a nervous virgin like me. The only reaction I got from my girl was a couple of moans, and they were not moans of pleasure.

Despite our disappointing first go at sex, Cathy and me got along well and started going steady. She lived in a really nice area in Winstanley and if I was rugby training after school, I'd catch the bus up there and see her afterwards. A couple of weeks into our relationship, I had two surprises in my bag to show off to her. First, I had won a trophy at rugby and second, I had in my bag a porn video given to me at lunch break by my mate Closey. He said it was the best one he'd ever seen – quite a compliment from a lad who must have seen hundreds – and I thought I'd see if Cathy was up for watching it with me. I arrived at her parents' posh four-bed detached house, gave her a kiss hello, showed her my trophy and stuck it on the sideboard with the video, which I reminded myself to watch later. We listened to music in Cathy's room and then went downstairs for some tea with her mum and dad. Afterwards, I said bye to everyone, grabbed by bag and sprinted off to get the bus home. It was only as I got close to our house and thought about showing the trophy to my dad that I realised it was still on the sideboard in Cathy's front room... along with the porno!

Luckily, Closey had recorded the film over an old Deanery school rugby game, meaning it was just a plain VHS tape like the ones everyone used to record stuff off the telly. I thanked God that it wasn't an original version bought from a sex shop, with a cover depicting its graphic, hardcore contents. I assured myself that I'd simply ring Cathy in the morning and ask her to bring the trophy and the tape to school with her. No one – especially her well-to-do, straight-laced parents – would be any the wiser.

I got home and watched TV with Dad and our Karl. About an hour later, there was a loud knock at the door and Dad went to answer it. 'This is your son's video,' ranted Cathy's dad, brandishing the tape. 'It's porn and it's disgusting.' He then handed it over, along with my trophy and Dad – who couldn't have been less bothered – just said 'Oh right, cheers' and watched him and his wife storm off to their car. It turned out that Cathy's folks, both rugby fans, had seen 'Deanery v Hull' written on the label and decided to play it. They got what they expected for the first few minutes until it suddenly cut away from school kids running around to a full-on, anything goes skin flick. I saw it afterwards and it was a really bad one, featuring positions you wouldn't think possible and some eye-watering sado-masochism thrown in for good measure. Prior to watching that, I don't think Cathy's mum and dad had seen anything more risqué than *Bergerac*. They were fuming and they banned Cathy from seeing me. Of course, being banned from seeing each other just made us stronger and we continued going out for a few more months before eventually splitting up when we both got a bit bored of each other.

Once the losing-my-virginity box was ticked, there was still an important rite of passage I'd yet to experience – getting drunk! And it turned out to be another rather embarrassing episode. Shortly after splitting up with Cathy, I went with Owen and a few of the lads to a party hosted by a girl from school we all called Big Karen. Her parents were away at the time and the place was a state when they got back. We got one of the older lads to go to the off licence for us and we each bought a bottle of Merrydown cider and a can of lager. It's all a bit of a blur but I recollect drinking all my booze before we got to the party, followed by some punch while we were there. What I do remember vividly is waking up at Owen's house in the early hours of the following morning having pissed the bed. I began to wonder what it was about the beds in Owen's house and me making a bloody pillock of myself!

But while my performance on the booze and babes

front was below par, when it came to rugby, everything was going great. I had success with St Jude's on the club front, Deanery High at schoolboy level and representative honours with Wigan town teams, the County and North West Counties sides.

By May 1992, I was 15 and I'd finally caught up with the other lads physically. I'd spent a couple of years wondering when I was ever going to get bigger but by '92, I'd filled out, got hairy bollocks and, boy, was I rapid. I'd never been slow but I suddenly had some proper pace. That year, Deanery High swept the board. At our age group we'd won Wigan Schools League, the Wood Cup, the Wigan and District League Shield and were North West Counties English School Champions. And the following year we did it all over again. In the English Schools Final at Wilderspool, Warrington, we beat Leigh's Bedford School 24-16. I was on top of my game that day, scoring a hat-trick of tries and grabbing a personal points tally of 18. And then to cap it all, me and my St Jude's mate Keiron 'Kez' Cunningham were selected to play for the England Under-16s against the French Cadets at a ground I would come to know so well: Knowsley Road, St Helens.

The big break I'd dreamed of came when I signed for Wigan. I was 15 but it wasn't made public until I was 16, when I left school. At one time I thought I was never going to get spotted. While scouts from Warrington and Wigan picked off other lads, I was overlooked. I knew I was a decent player – better than others who were being signed – and it was really frustrating. Then a bloke called Keith Mills, who was working at Wigan at the time, spoke to the scouts there and said: 'You're missing the best one, he's called Sean Long and he plays stand-off at St Jude's.'

One of them came to see me and said: 'He's too small.' But then another scout, Johnny Jackson, came and watched me in a game against Widnes St Marie's. I scored two tries and set up about three so Johnny asked me to go down to Central Park for a chat. He said they were looking at offering me a contract and I was ecstatic. But nothing was definite yet.

Being the wheeler-dealer he is, my dad pulled a fast one. He rang Wigan up and said we had a meeting with Dougie Laughton, the coach at Leeds, and blagged them that I was going to take a look round. I was never going to sign anything but Wigan didn't know that. They got me straight down and offered me a deal, £18,000 over three years. On Dad's advice, I turned it down and walked away. I remember thinking it was a huge gamble but it paid off. They upped the deal by a couple of grand and an extra year. Dad said: 'Always turn down the first offer on the table. You need to look after Number One.' And he's right.

I was still only 15, so I carried on playing for St Jude's. But the following year, when my birthday arrived, Wigan announced my signing and I was the happiest 16-year-old on the planet. I'd always told anyone who'd listen that one day I'd pull on a cherry and white shirt; it was my dream and it came true. Wigan chairman Jack Robinson said that my arrival was on a par with when the club had captured Shaun Edwards. That was praise indeed.

I started as an apprentice. Back then it was tied into YTS, the youth training scheme, so the government coughed up part of the money. You got paid £35 a week for training during the week and on top of that, you got your match money. If you played for the academy it was £35, if you played for the reserves you got £90 and if you played for the first team you pocketed between £400 and £450. It all built up from there. I played a few academy games and then went straight into the reserves so I was bringing home good money. Sometimes I played for both and was bringing home more than my dad! When I started for Wigan I gave Dad £15 a week board, but when I began bringing in more than him, he suggested I gave him £50. I declined the offer – after all, Dad's always told me to look after Number One!

By the time I was 17, I looked old enough to get into all the pubs and clubs and I was living the dream. I bought a car – a Corsa GSi flying machine – and loads of posh togs and I was out all the time. I went out a lot in Wigan with my old mates but when I wasn't with them, my going out pal was Wes Cotton, a fellow apprentice at Wigan who went on to become a great player and a very pretty fashion model! Wes and me hung out with some of the senior lads like Martin Offiah, and we all went to the famous Hacienda in Manchester most weekends. Like I said, I was living the fucking dream!

Martin was a great bloke and when we did our speed sessions in training he'd do it with us, even though we were just the YTS lads. I'd have races with him and he always won. He was as fast as anyone who's ever played the game. I would love to see him and flying machine Darren 'Alby' Albert in a race.

Shortly after my 18th birthday, Wigan asked me to

sign a new contract. At the time, there was a rugby league war going on between Super League and the National Rugby League. Wigan said that if I renewed my contract with them for the Super League I'd get a loyalty bonus of £20,000. That's right, *twenty bloody grand*! The answer was a loud 'YES!' The same amazing deal was given to Craig Murdoch, Kris Radlinski and Simon Houghton. They probably spent theirs wisely, investing in property or stocks and shares. My cash went on booze and birds.

In fact, that £20,000 went to my head a bit and I went a bit crazy. You can read about the worst bits in the next chapter.

CHAPTER 4

WIGAN BAD LAD

In common with most blokes, I like a beer. And I've probably had more than my share of bother as a result of the demon drink. But of all the drunken situations I've found myself in over the years, there's only one incident I truly regret.

It was a Thursday night in August 1995 and I was out in Wigan with a gang of players. Andy Farrell was there and so were Jason Robinson and Gary Connolly. We ended up at a club on the outskirts of town called Mirage, where a lot of the rugby lads used to go.

By the end of the night, I'd downed five or six pints of lager and a few shots of vodka and I was well drunk. It's hardly legendary boozing but I was only 18 and new to drinking. My tolerance levels weren't what they are now. Anyway, I rolled out of the club at around 1am and staggered into the road and into the path of a car full of girls. Despite my best efforts to charm them by dancing inches from the bonnet and making gorilla impressions, they were blasting the horn for me to get out of the way. They were also yelling at me – far more angrily than the situation warranted, I thought – and waving me out of the road. But back then I was nothing if I wasn't an annoying drunk so I stood my ground, waving back at them and pulling faces.

Then the driver started slowly edging the car towards me with the girl in the passenger seat reaching over to keep braying the horn. Their anger just made me want to wind them up more so I dived onto the bonnet. Oddly enough, none of them saw the funny side and all four of them piled out of the car.

I got off the bonnet and they all started having a go at me, getting more and more pissed off every time I laughed and told them to calm down. One of girls was well drunk and she gave me loads more abuse than her mates. She started pushing me and I was like, 'Hey, what are you doing?' I knew I'd been a pain in the arse but it was all just high spirits; I wasn't prepared for things to get this nasty with a bunch of girls. Then she totally lost it and began punching me again and again.

Next thing I knew, I instinctively swung back at her. But as I threw the punch, the girl who'd been driving stepped in to drag her mate off me. My fist ended up landing square on her chin and she dropped to the floor like a sack of spuds. I thought, 'What the fuck?' One minute I'm doing gorilla impressions, the next I'm decking some lass. I'd never hit a girl in my life and I was mortified.

Panicking, I legged it up the road to get away from it all. But I was chased by a group of lads who had seen me hit the girl. They caught up with me and I was cornered. I tried explaining that I'd been punched about a dozen times before hitting back, but my words fell on deaf ears and we ended up fighting – again it was four to one.

I held my own for a minute or so and landed some decent cracks but they soon got the better of me. As I stepped backwards from one punch, I twisted my left foot on the kerb and I could feel something pop. I went to the floor, rolling around in pain while the vigilantes kicked me. I remember thinking at the time, 'Talk about karma, you do something wrong and you fucking get it straight away.' The lads left me alone when they realised the pain I was in. I think they figured I'd had enough.

Rob Smythe and Ian Talbot, who were in the academy with me at the time, ran up to help me but by then the lads I was fighting had got back in the car and driven off. My ankle had swollen up like a balloon and I couldn't put any weight on my left foot. So they helped me into a taxi and Rob came with me to Wigan Infirmary to get it looked at.

Once we'd waited a few hours at A&E, I was taken over to one of those cubicles they have at hospitals with paper curtains. I was sat on the bed, telling the nurse, 'It's killing me, it's killing me.' Understandably, she was unsympathetic. She had the tone of a woman who was thinking: 'Here we go, another young pisshead.' She examined my ankle and said she'd organise an x-ray to see if it was broken.

Then, just as she finished speaking, I heard a familiar girl's voice coming from a cubicle across the way. She said something like: 'Yeah, yeah there's this lad, he hit me, he threw this punch and he hit me.'

Before I had chance to say a word, the nurse drew the curtains back. Suddenly, I was sat facing the girl I'd punched but she didn't notice me. Then her nurse said to her, 'Do you know what he looked like?' and, as if sensing I was there, she glanced towards me, jumped up and pointed: 'That's him, that's him!' I looked to Rob, who was sat on a chair beside my bed, and said: 'OH, FUCK'. Without saying another word, we did a runner – or, in my case, a hobbler. We went straight past the girl and out of the A&E doors. Luckily, there was a taxi dropping someone off so we jumped in and made our escape.

I woke up the following morning fully clothed, with a headache and a throbbing ankle that looked like a fat black pudding. I thought to myself: 'What the fuck was I doing last night?'

I knew something bad had happened but I couldn't for the life of me remember what. Then it struck me like a punch in the stomach and I felt sick. It was all coming back to me in flashbacks...jumping on the car bonnet...the argument with the girls...hitting one of them! I was frantic! 'What have I done? What will the gaffers at the club say? Will they find out?' I reasoned that they probably wouldn't find out. After all, the girl didn't know me from Adam so I'd be fine if I just kept out of Wigan town centre for a while. Keep my head down and I'd be all right.

My ankle was bruised and hurting but I was able to drive to the club at Central Park to get it checked out by the physio. I told him I'd tripped on a kerb (no lies there) and he said I'd done my ligaments and ordered me to spend the next four weeks in a cast until it was fixed. It was a bit of a pisser, but at least no one knew what had happened the night before. Or so I hoped.

I spent the next few days milling around the club, exchanging banter with the lads and earning my wage by cleaning boots and helping out with general stuff. I still had to work for my £30 a week, bust ligaments or not. Then, four or five days after the girl-punching incident, Mary Sharkey, the secretary – who went on to become a director of the club – came over and said there was a phone call for me.

'Is that Mr Long?' the caller asked. Immediately, I knew it was a copper and my legs turned to jelly. 'Yeah, that's me,' I replied, trying to hide the fact that I was shitting bricks. He told me I was required down the station about an incident the previous Thursday and asked if I could get there that afternoon. I made my excuses to the club and got myself there.

Once I was at the cop shop, they asked me if I had a solicitor. I said I didn't and the guy said: 'I think you should get one.' I was in trouble, big-style. I was arrested for GBH with intent. The police knew it was me who broke the girl's jaw because I gave my name and address when I went to hospital on Thursday night. The policeman who interviewed me was a right mean bastard – think *Life On Mars* cop Gene Hunt's harder, meaner brother.

And it got worse. Unfortunately for me, in between the girl-punching incident and the situation I was now in, me, Martin Offiah and some of the other Wigan lads had all dyed our hair silly colours. It was a daft bet before the start of the season and as I sat before 'DCI Hunt', my hair was bright red – and spiked up for good measure. As I didn't have one myself, the duty solicitor was called in to sit with me for the interview. One of the first questions the copper asked me was whether I had dyed my hair in an effort to disguise myself and avoid being identified as what he called the 'drunken thug' who broke the girl's jaw.

I explained the craic with the lads but he was having none of it. And to be honest, I don't blame him. He was dealing with the case of a girl who'd been seriously assaulted – why shouldn't he give me a hard time? I wasn't sat there feeling wronged, I just wondered how the hell I'd got myself into such a situation. I was out of my depth, really scared and thinking the worst.

The police had statements from the four girls that were in the car. When they were read out I felt sick. Apparently, I was urinating against the nightclub wall before I stumbled into the road. I also snapped the aerial off the car when I was sprawled all over the bonnet. Unfortunately, none of them said that I accidentally hit the sober driver while swinging at the drunk one who'd been punching me. I said: 'No, it didn't happen like that. I was sober, I only had a couple of pints.' The duty solicitor looked at me with eyes that said: 'Is that the best you can offer?' I looked back with eyes that said: 'I'm fucked here, aren't I?'

They charged me with a Section 18 – grievous bodily harm with intent – and it carried a maximum sentence of ten years in jail. I was allowed to go home but I was bricking it, really bricking it. 'Would the club have to know?' I asked myself. Then it dawned on me: 'They know already, you dickhead. They took the call from the cops!'

The next day I was summoned to the boardroom at Central Park, where the gaffers were sat waiting for me. Three directors, including chairman Jack Robinson and vice-chairman Tom Rathbone, along with John Martin, were lined up in front of me. I limped in there with my drinking injury, a few brawling marks on my face and my daft new haircut. The looks on their faces said it all but thankfully my dad came along with me for moral support.

They'd heard that I punched a girl outside a club at the weekend, breaking her jaw. Hearing it said out loud in front of my dad made me feel terrible, but I'd already explained to him what had happened and, although he was far from being happy with me, he was on my side and he believed I didn't mean to do it. The suits had a right go at me, asking me why I had to be so wild and out of control. They were saying to Dad: 'Why can't he be like Craig Murdoch? Why can't he be like Kris Radlinski?'

The lads the Board were preaching on about were in our team and were good players. They were sound blokes too, but I knew even back then that I just didn't have the same mentality as them. My dad stuck up for me, saying that if they took the daft and unpredictable side of me away they'd be left with less of a rugby player. I remember him saying that I was a bit random and a bit off the wall at times but that it was that side of my personality that gave me an edge on the pitch. He said: 'He's unpredictable and that's how he plays the game.' My dad believed in me and he stuck up for me. He has looked out for me like that since I was a little lad at St Jude's. Without him, I wouldn't have become the player I did.

The Board could have sacked me but they didn't. Instead, they ordered me to calm down and stop all the partying. I was keen to do whatever they wanted and I ended up joining a God Squad with some of the lads who played for the team. The God Squad was mainly made up of Kiwis; guys that were a good few years older than me like Va'aiga Tuigamala, Apollo Perelini and Vila Matautia (he was a giant of a bloke, hard as nails – you could be a full-on atheist and if he said you believed in God, you believed in the bugger). Then there was Jason Robinson (a bit of a bad lad before he saw the light) and a bloke called John Strickland, who was head of the God Squad and held the meetings at his house every Tuesday night. Basically, the Board had gone to the born-again boys and asked them to take me under their wing before I ended up on the dole or, worse, behind bars.

Believe it or not, I got quite into it and went along to John's house most Tuesdays for three or four months. But looking back, it was bloody weird sometimes. Typically, we would all have a meal (the Kiwis were great cooks) and then the guitar would come out and we'd have a singalong about Jesus. I quite liked that part of it and I enjoyed the good vibes but it had its odd moments. Occasionally, we'd finish a song and someone would say, 'Right, we're going to pray for Sean now', and they'd all put their hands on my legs and on my head and pray for me. I felt like the girl from *The Exorcist*! At other times, one of them would stand up after a song and talk about how they found God and then tell their story of becoming born again. I never did any of that speech stuff; I was there to stay out of trouble and eat the food.

Despite staying out of the heartfelt speeches and stuff, I found myself getting more and more under the spell of it all. But after a while, I began to feel really uncomfortable with it. All the God Squad lads were great people and I know they only wanted the best for me, but in the end I felt they were trying to take over my life; that I was being brainwashed. Some of them tried to turn me against my mates who I'd known since school, saying they were a bad influence on me for encouraging me to go out drinking and stuff. They were asking me things like, 'Why do you need to go out on a weekend?' and, 'What do you think God would make of all this drinking and partying?' By then, I wasn't boozing much at all, but they were still laying the guilt trip on me just for seeing my mates now and again. I explained that sometimes I'd be sat at home and the lads would ring me and ask if I fancied a pint to get out of the house and have a laugh. But they were still making me feel guilty.

I told my mates over a couple of pints what the God Squad guys had said. Owen and Tank (so-called because he used to wear a head guard with 'Tank' written on it) were, and still are, my best pals, and they couldn't believe what I was saying. Owen said: 'Shut the fuck up, Longy. We're your mates, we're just trying to cheer you up.' He confirmed what I already knew, that I was being a bit brainwashed. I gave up the God Squad and stuck with my old pals, the lads I knew best and who knew me better than any of the born again boys ever would. The God Squad had done me a lot of good and I'd calmed down loads but it was going too far. I didn't go to any more meetings after that.

Five weeks after busting my ligaments, I had the plaster taken off my foot and I was chuffed to bits. Having it on was a constant reminder to me and everyone else of the girl-hitting incident. I prayed that everything was going to be good from now on. But it turned out my prayer was about as much use as Professor Stephen Hawking in a Mexican Wave.

I'd been back in proper training for about a fortnight when I played in a reserves match away at Hull, the first game of the season and my first match since the injury. I'd had a clear season and I'd been looking good in training so they wanted me to play the first half of the game for the reserves and then bring me off to go on the panel for the first team. But they never brought me off and five minutes into the second half I ended up wrecking my left leg. I got the ball, dummied, went straight through the gap and when I got to the full back, the last man there, I went to step him. I was going full flight and I came off my left foot and he hit me at the same time. The pain was searing; I felt like I'd been shot. I took one look at my left leg and saw it was pointing in the wrong direction. I felt sick. I was meant to go off at half-time and now my career was over. I thought: 'Fucking typical.'

The physio, Keith Mills, came on and I was stretchered off. A few minutes later, the Hull doctor checked it out and said: 'It doesn't look too good, this, lad.' No shit, Sherlock. The next day, I had it looked at by the medical guys at Wigan and they confirmed the worst. I had three separate injuries. My medial ligament had snapped and come off the bone, I'd bust my cruciate and I'd torn my cartilage.

The doctors decided to try and get away without operating on the cruciate because it was such big job that took at least 18 months to recover from. Instead, they re-attached my medial ligament and trimmed my cartilage, hoping this would do the trick. But about eight weeks later, in early December, it went again in rehab. The physio was testing the power in my legs with a special pad I had to jump up from. As I landed either side of the pad, my left knee gave way. The quick job on my leg had not worked and there was no choice now but to get the cruciate done. I was operated on straight away and had to wear a brace for ages.

While my various injuries were blighting my life, I still had the GBH incident and the threat of going to jail looming over me. I was in and out of court for 10 months, pleading not guilty each time, because while I accepted that I'd broken the girl's jaw, I didn't agree with the 'intent' bit. The magistrates kept on adjourning the case every time I entered the not guilty plea, because the prosecution wanted more time to build their case against me.

On my third court appearance, in May 1996, my solicitor told me he was confident the prosecution would accept my admission of GBH without intent. He told me the maximum I could get for the lesser charge was six months in jail, but assured me he didn't think I'd get anything near as bad as that. He was confident I wouldn't go down. As we waited for everything to proceed, he nodded to the magistrates and said: 'Those three today are a lenient bunch, so let's hope the prosecution go for it.'

The magistrates asked the prosecuting solicitor if she

was happy with the lesser charge or whether she wanted it all to go to trial at Crown Court for GBH with intent. She was a tough-looking woman, a bit like Helen Mirren in *Prime Suspect* but not as fit, and she told the Bench: 'We would be satisfied with six months' imprisonment so we're happy to proceed today.' I thought I was going to faint. I looked at my solicitor and mouthed: 'What?' Did I hear that right? The prosecutor was talking as if six months in prison had already been decided. I looked at my solicitor and he shook his head as if to say she was talking bollocks. But his assurances did nothing for me; the scary woman for the prosecution seemed much more certain of my fate and I was bricking it. Six months inside? I didn't even have a change of clothes with me. Just my only suit, which had ripped when I'd stretched it over the cast on my foot. What a bloody nightmare.

Before sentencing, my solicitor told the magistrates that I was on the verge of a great career in rugby and stressed that I was a nice lad who made a stupid mistake. He told them how sorry I was and that I was absolutely mortified by the whole thing. There was no need to exaggerate because it was true; I was gutted. He did a great job and I felt sure that, whatever the outcome, he'd done the best he could. I was hoping against hope that they wouldn't jail me for the six months the prosecution seemed so sure of.

'Mr Long,' the Chairman of the Bench said. 'Yes sir,' I replied, in a shaky, sorry voice. He told me how drinking was the scourge of young people and that hitting a woman was a despicable thing to do. I nodded in agreement, giving him my best 'I know I deserve to hang for this but please be kind' face. He ended his speech by acknowledging my previous good character and remorse for what I'd done. My heart lifted and I thought: 'He's going to go easy on me.' He looked up from his papers and said: 'Taking everything into account, we've decided that twelve months...' He paused again as he shuffled through his papers while I bricked it big-style. I was thinking: 'TWELVE! That's a bloody year!' My heart was going crazy and I thought I was going to start crying. The prosecutor said she would have been happy with six months and these three coffin dodgers were meant to be lenient! I could kiss goodbye to my rugby career.

Then the magistrate looked up from his papers and added: 'It is a twelve-month conditional discharge and if you put a foot wrong in that time, you will go to prison.' He ordered me to pay £1,500 compensation to the girl and that seemed more than fair to me, as long as I wasn't getting banged up. In just a few seconds I had gone from being near-suicidal to wanting to run up to the bench and kiss all three magistrates. They were no longer coffin dodgers, they were fine upstanding pillars of the community and I loved them all. I could tell from the look on the prosecution solicitor's face that she was gutted. Ah, well!

I walked out of court feeling really lucky. I had come so close to going to prison and I was determined to stay out of trouble, if not just for me but for my folks and the gaffers at Wigan who'd given me a second chance. But you know what they say, best-laid plans and all that...

Three weeks after the court case, I went out for a few

quiet Sunday night pints with the lads at the Playhouse pub in Wigan town centre. Our girlfriends were also out that night but they were in their own gang; we weren't actually with them. We'd all made a loose arrangement to meet up at the end of the night.

When they rang for last orders, I was sober. I'd been skipping rounds and sipping my drinks, conscious of being bound over for 12 months. There's nothing like the threat of going to jail to keep you on your best behaviour. We'd had a good night and at about midnight we all went for a takeaway before getting taxis home. As we stood eating pizza at the taxi rank on King Street, we noticed some bloke arguing with my team-mate Nigel Wright's girlfriend. I didn't pay much attention at first but it got more and more aggressive and as I stood there watching it escalate, I thought: 'I don't fucking need this.' I'd only had three or four pints and I wasn't used to being so sensitive at the end of the night. I could sense things were going to get violent. Nige's girlfriend was getting more and more lairy and the bloke's mates were beginning to gather round. I was the closest of our group to the argument and watching quietly, hoping it wouldn't kick off.

Next thing I knew, the bloke had punched Nige's girlfriend, sending her flying over the bonnet of a cab and landing sprawled on the road in a right state. I was the nearest one to the bloke and my immediate reaction was step in. So I did, conscious of my bad left leg, and punched him to the floor. The irony wasn't lost on me. A few weeks earlier I was in court for punching a girl on a night out in Wigan. Now I'm flooring some guy for doing exactly the same thing.

The bloke's mates jumped in and me, Nige and some of the other lads started battling them in the middle of Wigan town centre. I wondered to myself whether I could have found myself in a worse situation if I tried. I was thinking: 'What have you done? You're going down for this, you'll get two years at least, you dickhead.'

But I was in the middle of a fight now and it was too late to walk away. There were about eight of us and about the same on their side. The punches were flying and I landed a few good ones but took a couple of hard hits too. A few minutes in, Nige – a big lad for a stand-off at 6ft 2in and around 15-and-a-half stone – singled out the bloke who floored his missus and took him away from the main fighting and down an alleyway for a proper pasting. I didn't fancy the guy's chances one bit.

Then someone shouted, 'The cops are coming!' and everyone scattered. I woke up on Monday morning a bit cut and bruised but otherwise physically fine (there is a lot to be said for not getting drunk the night before). But my mind was in overdrive with worry. If the police found out I'd been fighting just weeks after being handed a 12-month suspended sentence, I was going down.

I went to the club on Monday morning, feeling more than a little bit apprehensive. There were two possible outcomes from Saturday night's fight. Scenario 1 (the optimistic one): The bloke who got the pasting wasn't that badly hurt and that was the end of it. Though he might want revenge. Scenario 2 (the worrying one): He went to hospital and said he'd been beaten up by two Wigan Warriors players and the cops were sat in the boardroom with all the gaffers – and I was toast.

It turned out it was none of the above. In fact, I couldn't have predicted how it was to end up in a million years. Nige and me were summoned upstairs to see director John Martin. As I walked into his office, John was shaking his head at me in disgust. Ten months earlier he and the other directors told me to calm down and here I was in front of him again for fighting on another night out in Wigan town centre. John asked what happened and Nige explained that this bloke had punched his girlfriend, so I hit him and then a fight broke out. He admitted dragging him down the alleyway for a beating but said to John: 'What would you have done if some bloke punched your girlfriend?' I could tell John sympathised with Nige – after all, his girlfriend had been assaulted and why shouldn't he retaliate?

I was the one John was really pissed off with. While he was talking to Nige, he kept looking over at me like he was thinking: 'Why are you here, what are you doing, you fucking dick.' I'd been warned and I was in trouble again. I was about as popular as a cock in a bikini. I was expecting to be told to pack my stuff and get out but they had other plans. To be honest, when I decided to write this book I wasn't sure whether to mention what I'm about to tell because it will really embarrass the Wigan establishment. I debated for a whole five seconds before deciding 'Fuck 'em, I'm a Saint now and that's where my loyalties lie.'

John said that the bloke who took the beating needed hospital treatment afterwards. It turned out that John knew all about it because the guy was related to a local rugby legend. The man wanted £5,000, otherwise he'd go to the cops and the newspapers and tell them me and Nige had put him in hospital. The gaffer left it up to us whether we paid the bloke off but the message was clear. If he went to the cops, it would not be good for the club and it would not be good for Nige and me. Of course, I was the one who really needed to keep it quiet otherwise I was going to prison – no more suspended sentence let-offs for me. As far as I was concerned, it was a no-brainer.

John sent us out to make a decision and I said to Nige: 'I hit him first, you made a fucking mess of him, let's split it – two and a half grand each.' Nige was three years older than me and he earned a lot more money, although he had to retire when he was 24 after a horrific run of injuries. But he was nothing if he wasn't shrewd and he knew I was the one who stood to lose the most, so he insisted I pay £3,500 and he pay £1,500. I argued that he was the one who smashed his face in, but he just said that if it went to court he'd probably only have to pay the guy about a grand. The bloke had punched his girlfriend so it was hardly an unprovoked attack.

I, on the other hand, was in shit street and couldn't refuse the deal. To be honest, I'd have paid it all and then some to keep it out of court. If they'd asked me to pay 20 or 30 grand I'd have found the hush money from somewhere. So I sold my car – my beloved schoolboy racer Corsa – and came up with the cash. We gave cheques to the secretary at Wigan and they sorted the guy out from there.

I later heard that the police had found out about the fight and were desperate for the bloke to press charges against Nige and me. Thankfully, he needed the cash more than he wanted to see us done in court. In fact, on the Sunday night after we gave him the money, he was out in Wigan buying his mates loads of drinks to celebrate. My mate Owen saw them in one pub and they were raising their glasses and saying: 'Cheers for the beers, Longy!' He was loving it.

CHAPTER 5
I'M A SAINT

I was more trouble that I was worth to Wigan and they were fed up with me. They wanted me to be a clean-cut, well-behaved lad who didn't get into bother. Players like Craig Murdoch and Kris Radlinski were around my age and they behaved how Wigan wanted them to. They didn't go out boozing and brawling and causing embarrassment to the club. But I wasn't as bad as I seemed, I just always seemed to get caught. If there was a wrong place to be at the wrong time, you could bet your boots I'd be there. Whenever I did something bad, there'd be a director or whoever there to see it.

One time after training, I was driving home and some knob pulled out straight in front of me at a roundabout in Standish. I wound my window down and let rip with a stream of abuse. 'You fucking dickhead, you fucking cut me up!' I was waving my fist at him and going ballistic. It was rush hour and the traffic was really slow so lots of people saw me erupt. And, in keeping with

Longy luck, one of the witnesses was Wigan head honcho John Martin. I looked over, still red with rage, and he was sat in his car, shaking his head at me in disgust. He was obviously thinking: 'He's trouble that lad, he's giving my club a bad name.'

The Super League was born in 1996 and while I sat on the sidelines for Wigan, I watched St Helens top the table at the end of the season. In the first two campaigns there was no Grand Final, that didn't come in till '98, but I was very lucky to be starting my career at such an exciting time for the sport. I was back to full fitness and raring to go in the newly-formed Super League.

But my world came crashing down in the second season of the competition when Wigan got shot of me. They were looking to add some beef up front and targeted prop Lee Hansen from Widnes. To sweeten the deal, Wigan offered to throw me in along with 80 grand. I couldn't believe it and I was gutted. I'd never wanted to play for any team other than Wigan and the thought of moving to another club had never crossed my mind. But it was clear that my face didn't fit at Central Park, where even at full fitness I was behind Nigel Wright and Tony Smith, and the club were set on converting Kiwi Henry Paul from full-back to stand-off. Looking back, I find it quite amusing that Hansen made no impression at Wigan and was sold for bugger-all the following season.

I wasn't there to see the reaction of the decision-makers but, the way I see it, Wigan shelled out £80,000 to lose me, a Wigan-mad lad who would go on to become the only player ever to win three Lance Todd trophies. A shocked Andy Farrell said at the time that it would cost Wigan half a million quid to buy me back. But, as I've said, I reckon they were glad to see the back of me. I don't think they were worried if the move came back to haunt them.

As luck would have it, my old man was on the coaching staff at Widnes, where he was Dougie Lawton's assistant. I moved to Naughton Park in April 1997 and I was shocked by what a dump it was. The facilities were a joke, though I suppose I shouldn't have been surprised. I was going from what, at the time, was the biggest club in Super League, to a struggling outfit who'd seen better days and who were lying at the bottom of the second division.

It was a massive knock for me. Football fans took the piss out of Newcastle for dropping down to the Championship, but my move was worse than that. It was like going from the Premier League to a Sunday league pub team. We only trained part-time, with sessions on Tuesdays and Thursdays, which was a nightmare for a fitness freak like me.

At Widnes, the post-training catering was in the hands of an old boy everyone called Bepo – I never knew his real name. He was a sound old bloke in his mid-seventies who didn't even work for the club; he was a big fan who offered his services for free. After every session he'd turn up with a big jug of orange squash and cheese and onion butties his missus had made. And we're not even talking proper cheese; it was cheese spread with a bit of chopped onion mixed in. That was our official after-training meal. Don't get me wrong, I'm not a food snob – I know what goes into a doner kebab and I eat them sober – but I was used to nutritionally sensible fodder at Wigan.

Pasta, baked spuds, salads and energy drinks. To be honest, Widnes might as well have given us a Mars Bar each and a can of Tizer.

On the up side, the money Widnes were paying me was great. I was getting a basic £27,500 salary plus £1,250 a game. At Wigan, I was on the same basic but only £500 a game. God knows where Widnes found the cash. I played nine games in eight weeks so I pocketed more than £12,000 in the two months I was there. In those nine games we won just one – despite our excellent diet! But the joy of playing for Widnes was being able to shine as the stand out member of the team and after every game, people were asking about me.

The Super League scouts soon started to circle and I heard Leeds being mentioned and, of course, St Helens. It was exactly two months after I'd arrived at Naughton Park that Saints came to rescue me from my Widnes hell. I'd signed an 18-month contract with Widnes but the bosses kindly allowed me to meet with Saints. Widnes were losing game after game and having me was making little difference. There was a limit to what I could do in that kind of situation. I spoke to Graeme West and said: 'You've got to let me go, they're a big club. They've just won the Challenge Cup, I've got to go.'

Graeme wanted me to stay until the end of the season but he knew I needed to play in the Super League to develop to my full potential. He could have made it difficult but he didn't and I owe him a lot for that. Because I was only two months into my contract at Widnes, they understandably wanted a fee. They ended up selling me for £100,000 after getting me for nowt. Not a bad bit of business! And so it was, I went to

Saints. I was on less money than at Widnes – a slightly higher basic of £30,000 but back on £500 a game – but I wanted to play in the Super League and the pay cut was well worth it to be back in the big time.

As it happened, Widnes pulled their season around after I'd gone. They struggled but they made a couple of good signings with the money that they got for me. A lad called Jamie Bloom came in and started playing pretty well for them at fullback. I was chuffed for them.

It's funny how things turn out. When Wigan fobbed me off to Widnes I was gutted, but it ended up being the best thing that could have happened to me. The Widnes lads were a really nice bunch but they were far from a quality side. I don't want to blow my own trumpet, but I was out of their league. At Wigan, I was hardly getting a game and so had little opportunity to prove what I was capable of. At Widnes, I played every game and I was able to shine and that's how I came to the attention of the Saints. If I'd stayed at Wigan – way down the scrum-half pecking order – God knows what might have happened. And, looking back, I think the disappointment at being released by Wigan just made me more determined to succeed.

So, in June 1997 I joined the Saints, Wigan's deadliest rivals, and I had the chance to show Wigan in the most humiliating possible way just what a fuck-up they'd made in getting rid of me. My old St Jude's mates Kez Cunningham and Danny Arnold were at Knowsley Road and that helped make the transition easy. Shaun McRae was Saints coach at the time, but it was actually the club's Chief Executive David Howes who mentioned my name – which was just as well because Shaun had never heard of me. But the big Aussie took some time out to watch some tapes of me and decided I was the man to wear the Saints' number six shirt.

I remember seeing the Ceefax headline when I signed and it read: 'Former Wigan Bad Boy signs for Saints.' At the time Saints were up shit creek when it came to half-backs. Tommy Martin had done his cruciate and he was out. They'd just sold Lee Briers to Warrington and Bobbie Goulding had been banned. They needed someone. Apparently it was a two-horse race between Wakefield's Brad Davies and me. Luckily, they signed me and boy, was I buzzing.

I signed my Saints contract on the Friday night and turned up for my first training session the following morning at Ruskin, the place where Saints train. I was a bit nervous, like the new kid on his first day at a different school. And, after my first training session, I wondered what the hell I'd got myself into. We started running through some moves and it was going well with me in the scrum-half role. As we were running around I was saying hello to everyone and doing my best to fit in. When the session finished, I was walking back to the changing room and I got chatting with Alan Hunte. Alan had been at the club for more than a decade and he was a lightning-quick winger. I already knew him a bit and he was really sound with me.

We were having a good chin wag as we went through our stretches and warm-downs, when I saw Chris 'Moz' Morley throwing bits of mud at giant Samoan prop Vila Matautia. I remember thinking: 'That lad's got balls.' Moz was launching splats of soggy turf at the big man and they were bouncing off the back of his head. Vila didn't look too happy as he brushed the mud off himself while trying to work out where the barrage was coming from. Knowing what I know now, you really don't want to pull that kind of stunt with Vila. But at the time I didn't think too much of it and just sat down on a bench to take my boots off.

Next thing I knew, Moz came flying past with Vila hot on his tail. At Ruskin there are all kinds of leisure facilities, including a bowling green where a couple of the local pensioners were enjoying a nice quiet game of Crown Green. Moz and Vila raced past me and on to the green, still in their boots and ripping up the immaculate surface. Moz slipped and went over and Vila dived on him. Bang, bang, bang! The punches rained into Moz's face. He was on his back and squealing like a pig, trying to cover up, but Vila – who's 18 stone of pure muscle – was just flicking his hands away. The elderly bowlers looked on with their jaws on the floor.

Vila eventually realised he'd had enough and stopped beating him up. Nobody had tried to pull him off; it wasn't the kind of thing you'd do to Vila. You didn't mess with the big man. When Moz eventually got to his feet, he had cartoon-style lumps sticking out of his face and head. He was a right mess. A teenage Paul Wellens learnt that lesson the hard way in one of his first training sessions with Saints. Wello dummied Vila and went past him. The next move, Vila left a big gap and this time Wello went to step him. Vila just went BOOM, cleaned the lad out and, as the poor boy lay in a heap on the ground with birds twittering around his head, he said: 'Don't do that again.'

Wello hadn't done anything wrong other than

embarrass him. There were plenty of times in training when I could have stepped Vila but I soon learnt it was not worth the risk. The funny thing about Vila is he's one of many rugby players who are absolute beasts on the park but away from the game they're absolute gents. He's now a very successful property developer and I imagine that nobody ever tries to put one over him in the business world, either.

Anyway, after that eye-opening training session I made my debut in, of all games, a World Club Championship outing against Cronulla Sharks on June 16, 1997. A respectable crowd of 8,039 turned up at Knowsley Road to witness my first match in a Saints shirt. Sadly, we were on the wrong end of a hammering from the Sharks, who put in one of their best displays of the year. The Australians ran out 48-8 winners but I made a couple of good breaks and I managed to convert Alan Hunte's try.

The English teams were humiliated by the Aussies in that dreadful championship. We won just seven games to their 59! But that year, we learnt a lot about how the game was starting to be played. Gone forever were the days of big, immobile forwards thundering through the mud to make the hard yards before the fancy-Dan backs scored the tries in the final third. We were into summer rugby on hard grounds and that meant 13 athletes running with the ball, off-loading, kicking and chasing. The modern British rugby league player was probably born that season.

My Super League debut for Saints came in a 34-30 win at Oldham. It turned out to be a tough season for the club on the injury front but after the mauling we'd had in the World Club Championship games, we managed to reach the Premiership Final at Old Trafford – the last one before the introduction of the Grand Final. Fate's a right funny fucker because, as luck would have it, the opponents in my first major final were my old club Wigan. At the time they were still the biggest team in the game so it was never going to be easy. An Andy Farrell-inspired Wigan beat us 33-20 to pick up the trophy they'd also lifted the previous season. Losing to Wigan hurt like hell, but I ended my first season as an established Super League player. I did well enough that year to get picked to play for Great Britain against Australia. I was confident that things were just going to get better and better – especially if they were bad for Wigan Warriors!

My hometown club had rejected me and St Helens, the old enemy, had come to my rescue. When Wigan flogged me to Widnes it made me feel like I was a shit player. That deal put a serious dent in my lifetime love affair with my hometown club. As far as I was concerned, they could go and fuck themselves. I was seething and it's a fury that's played a part in every game I've played against Wigan since then. It's been my life's work in a Saints shirt to rub Wigan's noses in the shit at every possible opportunity.

Playing for Saints, just a few miles away at Knowsley Road, makes everything I've achieved even sweeter. Local rivalries are what makes competitive sport so special. Good Friday in east Lancashire, when Saints and Wigan traditionally meet, is a massive date for fans of both clubs. A win, and especially a good win, hands the successful fans bragging rights for weeks to come.

Any sports fan knows the true value of a derby win. In many ways, it's even better than winning a title or a trophy because you can go to work or school the next day knowing there'll be a few rival supporters to rip the piss out of.

But if I'm totally honest, I'll always have a soft spot for Wigan. After all, I was born and raised in the town and I still live there. All my mates and relations are pie eaters! If it was Wigan against Leeds in the Challenge Cup Final I'd be cheering on my hometown. As a Saint, I've spent 12 years trying to fuck them over, but as long we're doing okay, I'm happy to see a smile on the faces of my mates when they come away from the JJB having beaten Bradford, Salford, Huddersfield or any other bugger! But, of course, when I move to Hull, I'll be out to smash Wigan every time we meet. And when they play Saints, my loyalties will NOT be with the cherry and whites.

CHAPTER 6

LANCE TODD AND ME

May 4, 1985, saw the best Challenge Cup final ever, in which Hull, 22-8 down early in the second half, staged a valiant comeback, only for Wigan to hang on for a thrilling 28-24 win. The famous match is remembered as the Kenny-Sterling final after the two great Aussies who played absolute blinders. And I, a rugby-mad eight-year-old, was at Wembley that day to see it. When Brett Kenny took the Lance Todd man-of-the-match trophy and held it above his head, I decided then that I wanted to do the same.

I was back at Wembley in 1988, the year Wigan started an amazing run of eight straight Challenge Cup wins with a 32-12 hammering of Halifax. I was on another magical trip to Wembley with the family, breathing the same air as Wigan greats like Joe Lydon, Shaun Edwards and Ellery Hanley. Santa could stick Christmas up his arse; this was the best day of the year.

For me, the Challenge Cup final has always been the

game of the season, bigger even than the Grand Final. In the days before Wigan made the Cup their own, I had always watched the game on telly regardless of who was playing. But from '88 onwards, every spring it was time to head south to Wembley. Sometimes it seemed like the whole bloody town was down there. It was a belting day out.

I got £1 off Mum and Dad *and* a quid off Nan and Granddad every time I got man of the match. And considering I played for St Jude's, the Wigan Town team and my school, barely a week went by when I didn't earn a few quid. I saved it up for weeks before the final and on the big day, I was out of bed at 6am to catch the coach with the family for the annual pilgrimage to the Twin Towers. It was always an entertaining and open match – that was what Wigan served up in those days – and every year with five minutes to go we'd listen out for the PA announcer: 'The winner of the Lance Todd Trophy is...' It was always one of my heroes, true Wigan legends. And as I stood on my seat, buzzing off the electric atmosphere, I'd think: 'That will be me one day – it'll be my name ringing round this stadium.'

A decade later, in 2001, my dreams came true when I played in my first Challenge Cup final. But it wasn't quite as I'd always dreamed it to be. First, I was a St Helens player and a Saint through-and-through. Wigan had let me go and they could fuck off. And second, we weren't at Wembley. Instead, we were playing on the hallowed Rugby Union turf at Twickenham. It was a massive game, the 100th Cup final, and we were desperate to win. St Helens lost to Batley in the first ever final in 1897 and we couldn't slip up on another historic day.

ove left: Newborn me with Mum on the top floor of Billinge Hospital Wigan. Good job I wasn't scared of heights!

ove right: Aged nine months and trying to stay on my feet before bed. me things never change!

low: Me aged four with my dad's favourite ferret which he called Adam t because of his stripe. His was a vicious bugger who once bit right into cheek.

Above: Aged two with Dad, who, by the look of this photo, wasn't much older than me!

Below: Me, our Karl, Mum and Dad at my Nan and Granddad's in 1982. Granddad took this photo and I got a clip for flicking the Vs!

Above: Me, my Spiderman wellies and my favourite ferrets ahead of [n]ight's poaching, aged about five.

[Be]low: My dad posing in front of the family Capri before driving home [wit]h some rabbits for tea.

Above: I was a huge Bugs Bunny fan, but I had no problem skinning his mates!

Below: Me posing with the night's supper, aged around four.

ove: Our Karl and me in matching stripy rugby tops.

ow: Me aged 10 with Wigan legend Andy Gregory at a St Jude's
sentation night. We've since won five Lance Todds between us.

Above left: Barry Owen (the lad who got me into rugby) and me at the Wigan Town Under-11s team presentation night.

Above right: Aged 11 and winning the cross-dressing competition on holiday in Majorca. My Nan and Granddad had taken our Karl and me away.

Below: My cousin Dean, me and my friend Martin with the Challenge Cup our Wigan heroes brought home to the local pub, The Kirkless, in 1985.

Me after joining
Deanery High in
the third year. I
went to that school
for the rugby, not
for the lessons!

Above left: My homecoming speech at Knowsley Road after we beat Wigan in the 2000 Grand Final. My message to the Saints: 'Thongs for the memories!'

Above right: Wes Cotton, Tank and me in Ayia Napa in 1999. I paid for that holiday with the dodgy two grand Wigan gave me. Cheers, Wigan!

Below: Me showing off my diving skills at the Saints pre-season training camp in Lanzarote in 2000. God, it's a hard life!

On the afternoon before the game, we took our first look at Twickenham. One thing struck me straight away – the in-goal areas were huge. At Knowsley Road you could park a small family car in the in-goal but the ones at Twickenham could accommodate a bloody aircraft carrier. Our coach, Ian 'Basil' Millward, had noticed, too, and I could tell his tactical mind was working overtime. Our stadium tour would pay dividends the following day but for now we were off to a nearby place called The Scrummery for lunch.

We were all sat round, eating pasta and taking the piss out of each other. Kez was opposite me and I said to him: 'See that bottle of Tabasco sauce? I'll give you 20 quid if you down the lot.' I was expecting him to say, 'Fuck off Longy, you dickhead.' But I had momentarily forgotten that Kez will do anything – and I mean anything – for money. He put down his fork, picked up the bottle and downed the lot. He even shook the last few drops out onto his tongue! I panicked, thinking I'd just put the best hooker in the world out of the Challenge Cup final. Basil would bloody murder me. I was relieved and staggered when the lunatic appeared to be utterly unaffected by it and demanded his 20 notes. As I passed him his winnings, I said: 'Jesus Kez, you must be made of asbestos.' Saying that, I don't know the state of his arse the following morning – it must have looked like the Japanese flag! On the morning of the game we got up, showered, had some breakfast and then chilled before heading down to Twickenham.

The Bulls were a team of bloody giants; it was like playing Shrek and his mates. And that was where that previous day's tour of the ground came in handy. Basil had clocked the massive in-goal areas and he told me to keep sliding the kicks through to get their ogres turning and tire them out. We knew that if we could steer clear of the strength of their pack and keep them on the hop then we'd have them.

After the usual on-pitch warm-up runs and stretches there was a big wait for kick-off. We had the National Anthem and the then Prime Minister, Tony Blair, came over to give us all a handshake. I remembered that the top man had sent us a congratulations card when we'd won the World Club Championship that January. As captain Joynty introduced me, I said: 'Thanks for the card, Tony.' He gave me his usual toothy grin and said: 'Pardon?' I replied: 'Cheers for the card.' Still grinning like a Cheshire cat but with a look of utter confusion in his eyes, he said: 'Oh, it was a pleasure.' He obviously had no idea what I was talking about or who the fuck I was. I doubt he even knew what sporting occasion he was at. I imagined him nudging his minder at the start of the game and protesting: 'That's handball!'

It was no mean feat beating Bradford. They were on top form and went on to win the Grand Final that year. But because the in-goal areas were so huge, they were much harder to defend. It meant I didn't have to be so precise with my kicks and I could really have some fun. It suited our attacking game no end but it was a bastard for the Bradford bruisers. We prised open their defence with a deadly aerial attack and I tortured them with short kicks close to the line, producing first-half tries for Kez and Tommy Martyn. It was piss-easy putting the ball through into an in-goal that was 30 feet deep. It was a good three times deeper than at most rugby league grounds.

Basil had taken one look at the conditions and the park and spotted an opportunity. He knew that if we could keep turning Bradford around – some of their players were like oil tankers – we could be through while they were still facing up the pitch.

In the dressing room at the break everyone was buzzing. We were doing a good job, following Basil's game plan to the letter. But my game hadn't all been about kicking and I'd made a couple of good breaks down the left and slipped inside passes to Joynty. I was defending on the wing so I was all over the shop; out wide and then attacking from scrum-half.

During half-time it started to piss it down and when we came out for the second half we were all drenched within 60 seconds. In that kind of weather you need your defence to be strong and ours was spot-on. The rain spoilt the game as a spectacle but we didn't care and neither did the fans. As the mistakes started to creep in we just kept to our game plan: kick it into the in-goal, keep defending and just wear them down.

It worked and we won 13-6. In the dying minutes of the game, as our fans whistled for the ref to blow for full time and signal the start of the celebration party, I wondered who'd lift the Lance Todd. I'd played well and I thought I had to be in with a shout. And then the announcement came over the Tannoy system: 'The winner of this year's Lance Todd Trophy is … Sean Long'. Those words I'd repeated in my head since I was a little lad were being said for real. My skin was tingling and I could have cried; I was that chuffed. When Tommy Martyn won the award against Bradford in 1997 he told me it was the best feeling in the world. When my name was announced across Wembley, Tommy ran over to me, patted me on the head and said: 'Well done son, you've done it.' I replied: 'You were right, Tommy – it's the best feeling ever.' I'd only gone and fucking done it! It was a buzz that would only ever be equalled by the births of my three kids.

When the final whistle sounded, I went mental. All the lads were slapping me on the back, congratulating me and then Basil ran on and gave me a big hug. The Saints fans were singing my name. I had never felt so fucking happy. Then it was up the steps to pick up the Challenge Cup. As we passed it round, holding it aloft, the Saints fans went wild. Then I was handed the Lance Todd trophy. I held it in the air and the Saints crowd sang my name: 'Longy! Longy!' I took one look at the names engraved on the base ... Brett Kenny, Kel Coslett, Alex Murphy, all legends of the game, and it all started to sink in. I thought: 'You've done it, lad. You've only gone and done it!'

We did the lap of honour and then headed back to pop the champagne. We'd completed an unprecedented treble that season by adding the Challenge Cup to the Super League title and the World Club Championship. As we jumped around, swigging bubbly from the bottle, an official from the Rugby League came in to take the Lance Todd trophy back. That's the way it works; you don't get it back till the following week at the presentation dinner. They're probably terrified that the winner will get absolutely shit-faced – which I did – and end up losing it, breaking it or pissing in it. The trophy is formally presented at the Willows in Salford on the Wednesday after the game at the Lance Todd Trophy Dinner.

As well as the Lance Todd, Basil named me the Coach's Man of the Match and I was given a big crystal bowl. It was an amazingly proud day for me. When we got back to the hotel – it was only a few minutes away in the coach – it was party time. I thought it would be a good idea to fill the bowl with Jack Daniels and Coke. I passed it behind the bar and they filled it up as requested and it cost me a bloody fortune, about £400. But I wasn't bothered. I was so happy they could have charged me four grand and I'd have still tipped them!

They had to bring in extra staff that night to cover the bar and we all ended up bladdered. Johnny Vegas – the comedy genius and great mate of mine – is a huge Saints fan and he was there, supping pints of Guinness like the black stuff was about to be declared illegal. I staggered to bed at about 7am and woke up about two hours later.

As I lay there, hungover to hell but deliriously happy, I remembered when Wigan beat Leeds 30-10 in the Challenge Cup Final in 1995. I was at Wigan back then – just a kid on the fringe of the squad – and it was a magical day. Us young 'uns travelled to Wembley that day with the reserves while the main team – full of my heroes – went on a separate coach. After the game, we were all buzzing, having won the Cup for the eighth time in as many years. 'I know those guys,' I thought to myself as they lined up to hold the Cup. 'And I'll be one of them soon.'

When the ceremony was over, me and the rest of the youngsters headed to the car park to get the coach home. As I walked along through the crowds, I spotted the First Team coach and I caught the eye of Joe Lydon, who waved at me out of the back window. I waved back, chuffed that he'd acknowledged me. Then he beckoned me over. I raced to their coach, hoping to get a chance to congratulate them all on another great win. I never imagined in my wildest dreams what was to happen next. Joe opened the emergency door at the back of the coach and whispered: 'Come on, Longy. Get in.' I knew I'd be in for a proper bollocking when they did the roll call on the reserves coach and found I wasn't there. But I couldn't have cared less.

I jumped on and all my heroes were there, getting drunk and pouring beer all over each other. Joe pushed my head down and ushered me onto the back seat where I hid under a load of coats. Then after about five minutes, when I was sure we were well out of Wembley, I jumped out and yelled: 'Wahey! You can't get me off now!'

All my idols were there – the likes of Martin Offiah, Kelvin Skerrett and Sean Edwards – and they all cheered when they saw me. I felt on top of the world and thought: 'How fucking good is this? This is the best day of my life!' I trained with them all and I was always floating around the fringes of the squad. They all knew me and I got on with them all. But I'd never seen them in a situation like this.

I joined in with the boozing and soon I was dancing and singing with the rest of them.

Anyway, back to 2001. The coach was leaving at 10am so I dragged myself out of bed, jumped in the shower and made my way downstairs to meet with the lads for a quick brekkie. I stepped out of the lift and into the bar area and the first thing I saw was Kez and Johnny Vegas, lashed out of their brains. They'd been up all night drinking and, in Johnny's case, chain-smoking. That man is a bloody legend, a real party machine.

I managed a bacon sarnie and half a brew before we were all ordered onto the coach to head back north for the homecoming. Forefront in my mind when I climbed onto the coach that morning was the brilliant journey I'd had with my Wigan heroes back in 1995. And because I'd won the Lance Todd, because this was *my* time of glory, I wanted to make our trip home just as fantastic.

We didn't better it, but I think we equalled it. The coach was full of booze and by the time we were on the motorway we'd all topped ourselves up from the night before. We sang the entire way home while having beer fights and all the usual immature shit you'd expect from a bunch of daft rugby players who've never had to grow up. I was so hammered I was crawling up and down the coach on all fours.

When we got back to St Helens, I was incapable of doing interviews or anything like that. I'd had precious little sleep and shitloads of booze – I was a drunker version of Freddie Flintoff after England won the Ashes in 2005!

The Challenge Cup is the trophy every rugby league player wants to lift. It's like the FA Cup used to be before football became obsessed with the Premier League and the Champions League. It's the pinnacle of a player's career and I've been lucky enough to win it with Saints on an unbelievable five occasions. But the year after my first Challenge Cup victory, I learnt the heartbreak of a Cup final defeat.

As we travelled to Murrayfield to play Wigan, our form was hotter than Kez Cunningham's ring piece after a bottle of Tabasco. We were going to wipe the floor with them. In the semi-final we'd travelled to the neutral venue of Wigan's JJB Stadium to play Leeds and whipped them 16-42 in what was probably the finest performance I'd been a part of at that time in my career. Wigan, on the other hand, looked unimpressive in their semi-final at Headingley, holding out for a mediocre 10-20 win over Castleford. Every Saints fan, every player and all the pundits expected us to wipe the floor with them.

But when we turned up for training near our Edinburgh hotel the day before the game, we got the shock of our lives. The training pitch was a disgrace. It was on a slope and the surface was heavily rutted. Lads were tripping over and rolling their ankles left right and centre. We'd have been better off staying at the hotel and having a run-out in the car park. It was blowing a gale and the session was, without doubt, the worst we'd had all year. It was a disaster, especially before such an important game.

As the training session came to an end, we were looking at one another and shaking our heads. I said to Scully: 'What the fuck was that?' But we were such massive favourites that we didn't really care. Kris Radlinski, Wigan's star full-back, had been in hospital all week with an infected foot. Everything was going against them and confidence was growing we'd win with ease. With our form and Rads out of action, what difference was one shitty training session going to make? All the difference in the world, as it turned out. Rads was declared fit an hour before kick-off and played an awesome game that won him the Lance Todd.

I had a nightmare, kicking like a schoolgirl. Both sides scored three tries but I missed all three conversions. Wigan skipper Andy Farrell, on the other hand, knocked over all his goals. It was one of those days. We lost 21-12 when everyone in the know said we'd paste them. I was mortified.

In the usual run of things, any game against Wigan is massive. But that anticipation wasn't there for us that day at Murrayfield. It was just another game to us, instead of the massive occasion it should have been. You can't sell yourselves short in a derby, it is a special game and if you don't go in fully committed then you're going to get beat. In the dressing room I didn't want to talk to anyone, I just wanted to sit there on my own with my head in my hands. Cocky sods that we were, we'd booked a massive party back at the hotel. Hey, we were going to need somewhere to celebrate a massive Cup final victory over Wigan, weren't we? So there was a right royal banquet laid on and loads of free booze. We were miserable and full of self-loathing for the first few pints but once we'd drowned our sorrows things seemed a lot rosier. As Homer Simpson once said: 'Beer is the cause of, and solution to, all life's problems!'

Thankfully, we didn't have to wait long to make amends for that embarrassing defeat. In 2004, we were facing Wigan again in the Challenge Cup final and, for those of us who'd played in 2002, it was the biggest game of our careers. We were still hurting after the Murrayfield shambles and there was no way we were going to sell ourselves short this time. Back then we'd been cocky because of form, this time we were confident because we were prepared – and there's a bloody huge difference between the two. Cockiness makes you lazy and lose focus, while being confident brings determination and the knowledge that if you do everything right you'll win.

That 2004 final (at yet another venue, Cardiff's Millennium Stadium) summed up where we were that season. We were playing great rugby, fired through with a will to win that got us out of all kinds of scrapes. So, running out on a scorching afternoon in front of a packed house, I knew we'd win. That was probably the best game I've ever played, both personally and as part of a team performance. The atmosphere was electric, the stadium was magnificent and I was in the zone. I felt like I was a second or so ahead of everyone else. I could see everything happening around me, where players were, where the gaps were opening up; it was a great feeling. Then, with a few minutes to go, I became one of a handful of players to be named Lance Todd winner for the second time!

We ran out comfortable 32-16 winners and we went crazy in the dressing room. We'd avenged 2002 and it felt sweet. But then, sod's law, I got called in for a random drugs test and had to provide a urine sample. As anyone who plays physical, top-level sport will tell you, peeing on demand after performing for an hour and a half is no mean feat. I sat there for ages, downing loads of water. I thought it was never going to come, but finally I managed to do the business. I walked back to the dressing room to continue the party, only to be confronted by a deafening silence and a total lack of St Helens players, coaches and officials. While I'd been sat trying to produce a jar of piss, they'd buggered off back to the hotel to kick off the serious celebrating. The swines! I made my way up to the top of one of the stands where I knew my wife Claire and my dad had been sitting. Fortunately they were still there, so I wasn't totally on my own.

The team had switched from the Vale Hotel to the Angel, right in the centre of Cardiff and only about 800 yards from the stadium. We started to make our way up Park Street and turned into Westgate Street. I was still smack bang in the middle of the biggest betting scandal ever to hit the game (you'll read the inside story later in this book) and some fans thought that the infamous Bradford bet was just the tip of the iceberg; that I'd been betting against my own team all the time. So as we walked along, me with my kit bag slung across my shoulder, there was a fair bit of banter coming my way and an awful lot was about the betting scandal. But it was all pretty good-natured and deep down I knew deserved some flak, so I couldn't blame supporters for being pissed off. But then one fan, a beer-bellied meathead from Warrington, got right in my face and started screaming: 'You fucking cheating bastard!'

He was going berserk, but I was on such a high after the game that I was happy to take it. But Claire wasn't quite so chilled and she gave him a right mouthful back. For once in my life I did the sensible thing and calmed her down, and we walked away. When we arrived at the Angel I got myself a pint and had a quiet moment to myself to think about what it meant to win a second Lance Todd. I'd become one of a very select bunch of players – Andy Gregory, Martin Offiah and Gerry Helme – who had won it twice (though Paul Wellens joined us after winning it in 2007 and 2008). If I could have bottled how I felt, I'd be richer than Bill Gates. To sweeten the moment still further, I had the gloriously warm feeling of having beaten the old enemy Wigan and laying to rest the ghosts of the Murrayfield nightmare of 2002. I joined the rest of the lads and we had a monster party that continued into the small hours.

We were back at Twickenham for the 2006 Challenge Cup final. We were meant to be playing at the new Wembley but it was way behind schedule and the stadium was still unfinished. It was Daniel Anderson's first final as Saints coach, and the day that I became the only player in the history of the game to win the Lance Todd trophy for a third time.

Huddersfield were our opponents and no-one gave them a prayer. We were expected to win by 30 points and we did, but the scoreline didn't reflect the hard-fought game. It was the biggest game in Huddersfield's recent history so we knew they'd come out firing. They threw everything at us in the opening half and we were knocked by their in-your-face defence. They scored a try after five minutes with Brad Drew accelerating away from dummy half and getting out a nice pass to Michael De Vere, who sent winger Martin Aspinwall over in the corner. De Vere added the touchline conversion and the Huddersfield fans were singing their hearts out.

Drew was having a great day with his kicking game, and kept us pinned back for long periods, but as the half wore on we started to come back into it. I put through a grubber that Jason Hooper just failed to touch before Willie Talau raced on to a Paul Sculthorpe kick that luckily rebounded off the foot of Steve Snitch. Jamie

Lyon's goal levelled it and then their first cracks started to appear five minutes before the 40-minute whistle when Jamie made a half-break and fed Ady Gardner, who cleverly deceived the Giants' defence to send me over for our second try.

It had been a really tough, competitive first half, but when we went in for the break we knew they couldn't keep that kind of pace going. In the second half, gaps started to open up and we ended up running in another five tries. It was a final where by the end I knew I was in with a chance of winning the Lance Todd. Everything had worked for me that afternoon and I controlled the game well. But I needed something else a bit clever to hear my name announced over the Tannoy for the third time. That something came with our fourth try. I had the ball and Paul Anderson outside me. I shaped to pass and then nipped through the gap. As I went to the full-back I could see Jamie Lyon about 20 yards away on my outside but I knew I couldn't reach him with the pass. So I punched a kick through and he scooped the ball up to score in the corner.

The man of the match was between John Wilkin and me. Wilko was a true hero that game after breaking his nose early doors in an accidental collision with our man-mountain Paul Anderson. Blood was pissing from the poor lad's conk and the medics struggled to stop the flow. But he wasn't going to let a bust nose stop him playing in the Cup final and in the end, he had a huge dressing wrapped underneath his hooter and tied round the back of his head. Despite looking like a gory version of Mr Bump, he really grafted for the team and his bravery was rewarded with two tries. He ended up being inter-changed throughout the game and spent a lot of time off the pitch. I reckon if he'd played more of the game, he'd have picked up the Lance Todd that day.

When the PA announcer made the call it was my name that rang out for the third time in a Challenge Cup final and I was ecstatic. We won 42-12 and everyone was knackered after the punishing first half. But I felt full of energy. Winning my first Lance Todd was the proudest moment of my career and winning a second secured me a place in the record books with some of the game's biggest names. But now I'd made history; the only bloke ever to win three of the fuckers! If I dropped down dead from partying that night, I could meet my maker knowing I'd done what no other rugby player had done.

The new Wembley was ready by the 2007 season and we were there for the Challenge Cup final. The build-up to it was immense. We were through and Wigan were sure to be our opponents as they went into the semi against French outsiders Catalan Dragons. But in one of the biggest shocks in the Cup's history, Wigan were smashed at Warrington. Thousands of Wigan fans had already bought their tickets for the final and so they all duly turned up at Wembley in brand new Catalan shirts. No disrespect to the Catalans, but finals that don't involve two big guns fighting it out are always a bit underwhelming. I know it sounds patronising but I reckon rugby league fans would rather see a Saints v Wigan or a Leeds v Bradford final. People want a hard-fought game where there's a lot of rivalry and pride at stake.

Everyone who wasn't a Saints fan wanted the French

side to win. It was a crap game and the crowd showed their boredom with Mexican waves from early on. But we did what we needed to do and ran out 30-8 winners.

In 2008 we were back at Wembley, our third year running in the Challenge Cup final. We were playing Hull, a team that had given us problems in recent years. They were rarely up there in the table but they always gave us a game. We'd struggled a few times at the KC and they'd run us close in the 2006 Grand Final.

It was a very fast, end-to-end game. We'd make a break, charge down the field, drop the ball and then they'd be off and running. It was a scorching hot day and a lot of the lads were knackered, myself included. But we managed to build a 10-0 half-time lead thanks to tries from Matt Gidley and Francis Meli. But Hull threw everything at us after the break and a Kirk Yeaman double, both converted by Danny Tickle, gave them a 12-10 lead with 15 minutes to go.

As we struggled in that second period I got my second wind and calmed down. We'd been playing with our heads in the sand and getting caught up in the emotion of the game, which, given our experience in Cup finals, was totally out of character. It was only when they took that lead that we relaxed and started playing our normal game. Although there were moments of doubt we knew we could do it. The boys were really sweet and nobody was silly enough to try and win it on their own. We showed what we were all about in that closing period because with a second try from Francis and a couple more from Wilko and Leon, we ended up with what looked like a comfortable win on the scoreboard at 28-16.

LONGY

Sometimes I can't believe how lucky I've been. Six Challenge Cup Finals in my career, five winners' medals and three Lance Todd Trophies. I reckon the Challenge Cup fairy likes me.

CHAPTER 7
IN BED WITH BASIL

Super League has done for rugby league what the internet did for porn. It fired the game to a massive audience, who were ready to get more of it. My career coincided with this revolution; the most exciting period in the history of the sport. I started out in the pro game the year Super League was born and I've been fortunate enough to reap the rewards that have gone with it.

The new structure rode in on the back of Australia's hugely popular Super League, which was bankrolled by media mogul Rupert Murdoch through his TV companies. In 1996, our game needed a revamp and with the help of cash from Murdoch's Sky TV it got it in the shape of the new format and a summer season. I signed with Saints in 1997 and there have been plenty of highs and lows. I've lifted cups and won man of the match awards but I've also had my fair share of nasty injuries and jarring defeats.

The 1998 season was probably my worst results-wise, but I was still a new boy, thrilled to be part of the team, and I loved every minute of it. I finally made the break as a first team regular at the start of the '98 season, inheriting the number seven shirt from Bobbie Goulding who, after a lengthy period out through injury, moved to Huddersfield.

But it was a few weeks into the season and the home game with Leeds in May when I was first paired with Tommy Martyn, the Saints' regular six. I knew straight away it was going to be something special. Over the next five seasons we developed an almost telepathic understanding. He and I worked well on all levels, whether it was helping Saints win games on the field or having a right laugh together off it. If I put a kick through, Tommy would be on the end of it – if he pulled my finger, I'd fart. We buzzed off each other and we were a great pairing. We were known as the Morecambe and Wise of Knowsley Road.

To people who aren't fans of rugby league and those with just a vague knowledge of the sport, I am probably best known not for my performances on the pitch, but for betting against my own club to lose against Bradford in 2004. However – and this is a big thing to share with the world – I'd done something similar before, with Tommy, back in '98.

At the time, I frequented the Dog and Partridge in Pemberton where Mick Dean, who played for Wigan back in the day, also drank a pint or two. Mick was mad into his betting and he was always punting big on horses and rugby. He knew his onions and he was one of the few people I've met who can honestly say he's up overall on the bookies. If he had a hot tip, you listened (after buying him a beer, that is!).

Anyway, I was stood at the bar one afternoon with my pals Tank and Poydy when Mick came over. He said: 'Now then, lads, I've got a question for you. Do you know what price you can get at the bookies on the first point of a Super League game being a drop goal?' Of course, it was a rhetorical question and I went: 'Go on'. He said: 'It's 120-1. I don't know who the bookies have doing their rugby odds, but whoever he is, he's a generous bugger. We can make some money on this, boys. What do you think?' I didn't need to think, I had pound signs in my eyes and one word was repeating loudly in my head: 'KERCHING!' Mick asked: 'What do you reckon, Longy?' I said: 'I reckon we'll soon be scoring the first point with a drop goal. You bet your fucking boots we will!' I did the maths; a hundred quid at 120-1 netted twelve grand. It seemed too good to be true.

So, the next day I went to training and I told Tommy what Mick had said. He's a good lad, Tommy, as honest as the day is long. But he's no fool and figured that if we weren't actually throwing the game, there was no harm in having a bet on ourselves. Obviously, I know now from experience that a lot of people don't see it that way.

We were playing Leeds away the following week and we put a plan together. The game was on the Friday night and so we agreed we'd place our bets the afternoon before. On the lunchtime, I drove round the bookies in Standish with a mate, getting him to go into each shop, waging a tenner at a time. I didn't want to arouse suspicion by putting a wad on at one place and thought it best that I didn't put the money on myself in case the bookie recognised me as a Saints player and smelled a rat. If only I'd exercised such caution six years later when betting on Bradford to beat us. With every bet we put on, the odds shortened. Tommy was sticking his money on six miles away in Leigh and Mick was doing the same up the road in Pemberton. The bookies clearly twigged there was something going on. After all, they probably went months without anyone placing such a bet and now it was happening dozens of times within a six-mile square area. Within an hour, the odds were cut from 120-1 to 6-1. The bookies clearly thought there was a sting going on – and they were right. I wagered a total of £70, at odds ranging from 120-1 on the first bet to 16s on the last. Despite the slide in price, I stood to make about three grand. Mick and Tommy were about the same.

Once the bet was on, the next job was to score the first point against Leeds with a drop goal. And it was no mean feat. Leeds were in belting form that year and playing them away was a rock-hard tie. Me and Tommy made a plan for the game. We decided we'd send a couple of drivers in and then I'd run in third tackle, get us a quick play of the ball then play it to Kez, who'd pass it to Tommy who'd then kick the drop goal. Tommy did all the kicks back then.

As I walked onto the pitch at the Headingley Carnegie Stadium, I caught Tommy's eye and gave him a knowing nod. This was going to be the most lucrative game of our careers. About four minutes in, it was 0-0 and we were awarded a penalty. Instead of going for the kick –

which to be fair was too far out anyway – we said we'd kick to touch, take two drivers in and I'd take the third, play the ball and then Tommy would drop goal. Simple as that.

So Tommy got the penalty, went to kick to touch but didn't find it and the Rhinos got the ball. Three seconds later, their left winger Francis Cummings scored in the corner. Fucking nightmare! Conceding a try early in the game is always a downer and every Saints player looked pissed off. But not as gutted as me and Tommy. Anyone watching our reaction would think we'd just been beaten in the dying minutes of the Grand Final! We'd both just lost thousands (well, 70 quid or so but we're talking potential winnings here) and I, for one, was almost in tears.

Despite the start of mine and Tommy's beautiful relationship, and the arrival of another Saints legend-to-be Paul Sculthorpe, the 1998 season was a dismal campaign for Saints. Wigan were a constant kick in the bollocks, knocking us out of the Challenge Cup and beating us three times in the Super League as we struggled to finish fourth. Shaun McRae paid for a season of under-achievement with his job and was replaced by Ellery Hanley, one of the true greats of the game. Ellery's arrival at the club in 1999 gave us the boot up the arse we needed and in 12 months we'd transformed into a Grand Final-winning outfit. I notched up 284 points that season, a pretty good return from my first full season as first choice scrum-half.

By the end of the 1999 campaign, I'd been at Saints for two-and-a-half years and I was still on 30 grand a year, the same money as when I started. When Bobbie

Goulding was shipped on, I found out that he'd been on £100,000. As I was his direct replacement as No 7, I wanted Saints to match my money to his. I asked for a rise and they offered me 60 grand and I said: 'No, I want what Bobbie was on.' I wasn't being greedy; I just wanted to be treated fairly. Saints was, and is, a very profitable club and I was doing well for them. I wasn't happy with the way they were trying to rip me off.

I had 18 months left on my contract and I wanted a new one for £100k. Wigan got wind of the trouble I was having and offered me what I wanted to go back to them. The problem was, I couldn't leave Saints until my contract ended, so I'd be stuck on £30k for another year and a half. My dad came up with a plan where Wigan would give him a cheque for two grand every month to boost my earnings, while I waited for my Saints contract to run out. The idea was that they'd give us the money to keep them in favour with me so I'd move to them. They were up for it and they said they'd pay the two grand to my dad every month and say it was payment for scouting for them. My dad would then give the money to me. Sweet.

I took one payment of £2,000 and then Saints found out Wigan were sniffing around to get me back. Ellery called my dad and asked: 'Are you having trouble with your Sean's contract, Bernard?' Dad pulled no punches and said: 'Yes, you've lost him, he's going to Wigan when his contract's up. He can't stay on with you if you won't pay him the going rate. He's got to look after himself, and he's going to Wigan in 18 months if you don't come up with what he wants.'

Ellery didn't want me to go, so he went into the

boardroom to see the tight arses who were refusing to increase my salary. He told them that I was one of his best players, with huge potential, and that they'd be kicking themselves if I went to Wigan. They listened to him and agreed to give me what I wanted. So, I signed a new contract with Saints and told Wigan: 'Thanks, but no thanks.' They rang me up and said: 'Where's the £2,000 we gave you? Can we have it back, please?' I said I was keeping it and there was nothing they could do about it. After all, giving me the money in the first place wasn't exactly fair play, so they weren't in a position to get heavy with me.

At around that time, we played Gateshead at home and I popped the AC joint in my shoulder. It's a bloody painful injury that can only be cured with rest, so basically my season was over. Ellery told me to have a holiday and so I rang round my mates – Tank, Owen and Wes – and asked if they fancied going away. They were all skint but that didn't matter. 'I'll pay,' I told them. 'I've got two grand off Wigan burning a hole in my pocket!' I paid for the four of us to go to Ayia Napa in Cyprus and there was enough left over to give them all spends. In the pub that night we raised a glass to our benefactors: 'Cheers, Wigan!'

We went away for a week and blew all Wigan's money on booze and birds. It was quite tame in comparison with holidays I've had since but it was still a riot. One of the lads, I think it was Tank, brought a hooter with him, the kind of thing you get on a clown's car. Every afternoon at 3pm sharp, Tank sounded the hooter to indicate it was time to get back on the lash. And so, we'd sit on the beach, supping cans of lager and checking out the talent. And bloody hell, what a great place it was for good-looking British girls wanting a good time.

We'd only been there for about five hours when we got chatting to four really fit girls from London. They had a game of Twister and we played it with them on the beach – oh, and they were all topless! Playing Twister with girls who are wearing nothing but skimpy bikini bottoms is an incredibly horny experience for randy twentysomething lads and I, for one, had some embarrassing activity going on in my shorts. But the frustration was short-lived because we ended up at it with them that night. The next day, we moved onto another group of girls from Wolverhampton. Again, we ended up bonking them, too. I had a different girl every day on that holiday – it was just what the doctor ordered!

When I got back, my shoulder joint seemed to have miraculously fixed itself – I put it down to all the shagging. While I was away, we lost 40-4 to the Bulls and now we were about to play a Grand Final qualifying semi against Castleford. As I was fit again, Ellery put me on the bench but I came on to score two tries and knock over five goals. Not bad for a bloke who a couple of weeks earlier couldn't carry two pints back from the bar.

Given my lack of match sharpness, I started on the bench again for the Grand Final but Ellery played me at the 24-minute mark. Again, Bradford were our opponents and they were winning 6-2 until Kevin Iro scored a try in the right hand corner to level it 6-6 after 65 minutes. It was up to me to kick the conversion with just a few minutes to spare. I was only young and it was the most nerve-racking kick of my career. Luckily, the day before the game I went to Old Trafford and I had a few practice kicks on the exact same spot I was at now and I was banging them over. I tried to pretend to myself it was like the day before, but obviously it wasn't – I didn't have 60,000 people watching me for a start!

But I managed to keep my cool and kicked it between the posts to win the game 8-6. Over the years, I have got pretty good at ignoring the crowd because it just takes one comment from a fan to take you out of the concentration zone. A Saints fan yelling, 'Come on, Longy' can be just as off-putting as a rival supporter threatening to kill me. I just switch off from everyone so that it's just me, the ball and the posts.

The 2000 season should have started with everything all sweetness and light at the club as we looked to build on that hard-fought Grand Final win. But a humiliating 44-6 loss to Melbourne Storm in the World Club Championship, followed by a 32-10 defeat at the hands of Bradford in the opening game of the Super League season, meant the club decided it was time to say goodbye to Ellery. It seemed a tough call given that just a few months earlier we'd won the Grand Final. But, in truth, I think he wanted out anyway. He didn't get on with the directors and he kept calling them 'dinosaurs' when he talked to the press. He was really vocal about not liking them. At the start of the 2000 season, Saints held a big bash where we wined and dined our would-be sponsors. Towards the end of the night, when everyone was making speeches and stuff, Ellery stood up and said to the sponsors: 'Be careful what you do with your money. Keep your money.' We all looked at each other as if to say: 'What the fuck?'

Once Ellery was gone, we needed someone who could put the polish on the amazing team spirit he had built. That person was Aussie Ian 'Basil' Milward, a relatively little known coach who'd been doing great things at Leigh Centurions. We called him Basil because he had hair the same colour as Basil Brush. Under Ellery, Tommy was on his way out and Aussie Darrell 'Tricky' Trindall had been signed as his replacement. But within days of joining us, Basil took me to the side and asked me who I wanted as my half-back partner. I said: 'Tommy every time.' Tricky was gone within a month.

Tommy and me were just the kind of half-backs Basil wanted. He could see through the fact we pissed around a lot of the time and he knew we had the talent needed to play his way. He was more than happy to let us go out on the park and express ourselves without trying to force a style of his own down our throats. The two of us put in some great performances both individually and as a pairing, but that season the side lacked the consistency that we needed to top the table. We ended up in second spot after a piss-poor performance on 15 September 2000, when we were hammered 4-42 at home to Wigan.

It was the last league game of the season, leading into the play-offs, and we were outclassed in front of a 16,000 crowd. We had a recovery session the next day and Basil wanted us there by 10am sharp. 'I don't want any absentees,' he said. 'So don't go drowning your sorrows in beer.' His eyes moved to me when he said that.

I gave him a nod and a wink that said: 'Don't worry,

Basil, I'll take it easy.' But the problem for me is I am always buzzing after a game and I can never get to sleep. I was living on my own at the time and if I went home I'd just be sat twiddling my thumbs until 4am, driving myself crazy. So, win, lose or draw, I always went out drinking after a match. That night, me, Paul 'Newy' Newlove and Chris 'Smiggy' Smith hit St Helens town centre for a few beers. Newy bailed out after a couple of pints, leaving Smiggy and me to it. We visited a few pubs before ending up at the Nexus nightclub. I was a bit pissed but still felt wired and wide awake. We stayed in the club for an hour or so, during which time I managed to crash and burn with two girls. I was never on form after a bad defeat, especially when it was a Wigan whitewash.

We left the club at about midnight and stood in the street, working out where to go next. Then Smiggy said: 'Newy is staying at the Hilton hotel round the corner so why don't we go there, wake the fucker up and have a bevy in his room?' Newy lived miles away up in Yorkshire and so he stayed in St Helens when we'd had a game followed by training the next day.

When we got to the Hilton I put on my best sober voice and said: 'We're from St Helens Rugby Club and one of our colleagues is staying here tonight. Can you tell us which room he's in, please?' I'd only had about six pints so I was just a little bit drunk. The bloke behind reception said there were two rooms booked by St Helens and he gave us the room numbers. They were both on the same floor and so we got in the lift and went up to see Newy. We tried working out which other player was staying at the hotel that night but it didn't matter, none of the lads would mind us diving into their rooms and terrorising them. Much worse happens on tour.

As we were going up in the lift, a porter got in with us and, as luck would have it, he followed rugby league and he recognised us. We blagged him that we needed to see our team-mates and he unlocked both of the rooms for us. The rooms were at opposite ends of the corridor, about six doors apart. I didn't know whether I had Newy's room but I didn't care. All the lads on that Saints team back then were game for a laugh and I was sure whoever it was wouldn't mind.

So there we were, stood at each door, synchronising our invasion. 'Five, four, three, two, one – GO!' We sprinted in, like half-cut SAS soldiers. It was pitch black and I could hear someone snoring so I just ran in, dived on the bed and went: 'Raaaahhhh!' I grabbed whoever it was underneath me, gave him a few light punches and said: 'Come on, fella, it's time to get up and raid the mini bar!' Then I heard this confused, scared, half-asleep bloke say: 'What's going on, mate? What the fuck are you doing, mate?' I was sat astride the guy, my hands on his shoulders, when suddenly I thought to myself: 'Hold on, I recognise that Aussie accent.' And then it dawned on me in a sickening rush: 'It's BASIL... THE FUCKING GAFFER!' At that point, someone lying next to him sat bolt-up in bed and screamed: 'Ian, what's going on? What on earth's happening?' Oh my fucking God, his wife was in bed with him. Even by my standards, this was a pretty awkward situation to be in. A few hours earlier, I'd been warned not to go out and get drunk before the 10 o'clock session in the morning.

And now I was sat astride the man who'd issued that warning and his wife was next to him, thinking I was Freddie fucking Krueger!

I jumped up off the bed and zoomed back out of the room. As I hit the brightly-lit corridor, Smiggy came running out of his room and he looked like he'd seen a bloody ghost. I thought to myself: 'What's wrong with him? Has Newy seen his arse over being woken up?' But it wasn't Newy in that room – it was Basil's teenage daughters! They told him who they were when he said he was looking for Newy. Could it get any worse?

Of course it could. It was pitch black in Basil's room but he must have recognised my voice, because as Smiggy and me stood panicking in the corridor, he yelled: 'Sean Long, what the fucking hell do you think you are playing at?' I did what I always do in such situations and legged it. There was no time to get the lift and so we hit the fire escape and sprinted down the stairs, through the hotel foyer and out into the street. 'He didn't know it was me for certain,' I told Smiggy. 'I'll just deny it in the morning.'

My heart was racing after that experience and I felt stone-cold sober and more awake than ever. I definitely didn't want to go home and worry myself to death. Luckily, Smiggy knew someone who was having a party – it was Friday night, after all. So we ended up going to this bloke's house, and I drank the various free spirits and beers that were available and got properly drunk. I woke up in the morning on the couch, surrounded by empty cans and overflowing ashtrays and thought: 'Where the fucking hell am I? What was I doing last night?' And then I remembered the hotel incident. 'I can't be late for training,' I thought to myself. 'I've got to let Basil think it wasn't me in his room.'

Smiggy had crashed out somewhere upstairs and he came down and somehow managed to blag the party bloke's car keys off him, telling him it was 'a matter of life or death'. So we sped off across St Helens to the David Lloyd gym where we were all meeting. We ended up being 10 minutes late and when I walked in wearing last night's clothes and stinking of ale, Basil was stood there shaking his head. He came over to me, tired and pissed off, and said: 'I want a word with you.' He then went back to his seat and talked to us all about the previous day's game against Wigan. We were playing them the following week in the play-offs and Basil said that we had to put the defeat behind us and concentrate on the next tie.

After the team talk, Basil took me to one side and gave me a bollocking. He said: 'What do you think you were doing going out and getting pissed after a dreadful performance like that?' I explained how hyper I feel after a game and that I like to get it out of my system with a drink with the lads. He seemed to accept that and I thought I was doing okay, but then he asked: 'Why did you jump on my bed in the middle of the night?' There was no point in denying it and so I told him that I thought it was Newy's room but he was having none of it. He knew Smiggy had invaded his daughters' room but he wasn't that bothered about him. His contract was up at the end of the year and they weren't renewing it. So Smiggy got away with it and I got the flak. Basil said: 'We're playing Wigan again in the play-offs next week. It's a massive game and you're getting drunk and jumping on people's beds. You need to grow up, Sean.' I knew he was right and I told him it wouldn't happen again. But at the end of the day, Basil knew what I was like and I don't think he was that bothered. He's a good bloke and he saw a bit of himself in me. I don't think he had it in his heart to give me a really hard time over some daft drunken prank.

After training that morning, I grabbed Newy in the car park and asked him where the hell he'd been sleeping. It turned out he was a few doors up from Basil's daughters and he heard all the commotion. After controlling his laughter, he said: 'I knew it was you and Smiggy and I just rolled over and went back to sleep.'

CHAPTER 8
IT'S WIDE TO WEST!

September 22, 2000, saw what rugby league fans recently voted the greatest try ever scored. It was certainly the most dramatic end to any game of my career. We were at home to Bradford in the Grand Final qualifying play-off. With just seconds remaining, the Bulls were leading 11-10 and the game was surely theirs. In those dying moments, as the whistles of the impatient Bradford fans rang in my ears, I remembered some advice Basil had given me. He said that if I found myself with the ball deep in our end with seconds left, don't just boot it down field. 'It's what they'll be expecting,' he said. I was about to put Basil's guidance to the test.

The ref called a penalty to us with just seconds to spare. But Bradford weren't worried – we were 80 metres from their line – and the Bulls fans were happily counting down the seconds. They didn't bank on the spirit of arguably the best Saints side in the club's history. Scully took the penalty and quickly passed to me. Immediately, the Bradford defence dropped back, waiting for the kick. Bearing in mind what Basil had told me, I turned to my right and kicked across the field. What happened next is the stuff of rugby league legend. In fact, the footage of it has become a YouTube sensation with tens of thousands of hits. We've watched it time and again at Knowsley Road and while writing this, I watched it again for the umpteenth time and I buzzed off it.

The commentary by Sky's Eddie Hemmings is an absolute classic and I could never convey the drama as well as him. So, over to Eddie:

'They are still not out of it [Saints]. They [Bradford] are taking a show on; they know they have only got ten seconds. Will they get this play of the ball? They are holding Sculthorpe down. Sculthorpe wants to get on with it. Bradford are counting down. Sculthorpe passes to Long. Long kicks it wide to Iro. Iro to Hall. Hall is trapped. Back it goes to Hoppe. Over the shoulder to Hall. There is Jonkers. There is Long. Long fancies it. [I run down the pitch] IT'S WIDE TO WEST! IT'S WIDE TO WEST! It is Dwayne West! [Dwayne sprints down the left wing, then passes to Chris Joynt] Joynt! Joynt! Joynt! Aaarghhh! Aaarghhh! Fantastic, they've won it! Chris Joynt has won it. It is unbelievable here, it is frankly unbelievable. What a run, what a try, what a match, what drama. I've never seen a try like that. The clock was up, there were only two seconds remaining! Saints can dig deep, but that was a huge hole. I'm pinching myself.'

We'd won it with two seconds to spare – the crowd went mental and so did the players. I looked up at Basil and he was ecstatic; he was jumping up and down like his Lottery numbers had come up. But the reaction of Matthew Elliot, the Bradford coach, is the one everyone really remembers. With a minute to go, he was smiling from ear-to-ear, chuffed to have got one over on us at Knowsley Road. But his grin steadily sloped downwards as we got closer to the try and when Joynty dived down with the ball to win the game, he literally fell off his chair! When you watch it back, he's there one moment and then disappears out of view the next. A classic example of a coach's world collapsing around him!

As the Bradford camp got their heads round what they'd just seen, we all jumped on Joynty – even our mascot St Bernard joined in the pile-on. In all the commotion, I pulled St Bernard's big furry head off to reveal a 50-odd-year-old guy inside. I couldn't believe it was such an old fella, I always thought it was a member of the youth team who came out every game to dance round like a lunatic. Anyway, he was loving it. He's a massive Saints fan – as you'd expect – and he was buzzing with it all. I was in full-scale party mode so I stuck St Bernard's head on and ran across the pitch. I wanted to take the goal kick with the St Bernard head on but the ref wouldn't let me. Anyway, back to Eddie Hemmings:

'Long kicks the goal, adds the extras. That is the icing. Chris Joynt's try converted by Sean Long. Saints have won it 16-11. The most remarkable match that you have ever seen. In Super League we have seen some outstanding games but none with the drama that we had here tonight. Absolutely breathtaking. Nobody in this crowd tonight or watching at home on television will ever forget the drama of that last minute. There have been some wonderful moments in the opening five years of Super League but few are going to match what we have just witnessed. The never say die attitude. They just would not give in. That was the most dramatic ending to a game that I have ever seen in my life.'

Eddie is meant to add drama to his commentaries; it's what he's paid for. But he wasn't exaggerating. It really was the most dramatic end to a game I have ever known. I have never known a crowd go mad like that – Grand Final or otherwise – and I'm proud to have been involved. I am still in contact with all the lads I played with in that game and we still talk about it now.

After that historic win, we went on to hammer Wigan 14-54 at the JJB to get to the Grand Final at Old Trafford, where we won 29-16. As always, St Bernard was there to share the victory and the old guy went nuts.

Funnily enough, in May 2009, just weeks ago as I write this, we played Gateshead at their place in the Challenge Cup quarter final and I was reminded of another crazy mascot incident. Before the game, I was at the end of the tunnel, checking out the pitch, when a Geordie guy came up to be and asked: 'Hi Sean, remember me?' I said: 'Sorry mate but no, should I?' Then he said: 'Why aye, I'm Captain Thunder, the Gateshead mascot.' Bloody hell, I remembered him now and all I could do was laugh nervously and apologise. Let me tell you the tale. It was 1999 – I'd been at St Helens for a couple of years – and me and some of my best pals (Owen, Tank, etc) went up to Newcastle for a lads' weekend on the lash. We went round the Toon on the Friday and Saturday, taking in the delights of all the lovely ladies on the Bigg Market. On the Sunday afternoon, Wigan St Jude's – the amateur side Owen, Tank and me used to play for – were up on Tyneside to play Gateshead Thunder in the preliminary rounds of the Challenge Cup. So we topped up the previous night's booze with a few pints for lunch and went to support our old team before catching the train back to Wigan.

We turned up expecting the tickets to be about a fiver but they were 15 quid a pop and we weren't paying that. Then I spotted the players' entrance and said: 'Follow me, lads.' We walked straight down the tunnel, onto the pitch and then into the stand where we sat down and acted like we were meant to be there. Nobody said a word. There were only a couple of thousand people in the crowd and it was hardly like we were taking people's seats.

And so, we were sat there, pricking around like you do when you're drunk, and someone from the Gateshead camp recognised me and came over. 'Hiya, Sean, would you do us a favour and come on at half-time and do the Golden Gamble draw?' I said: 'Yeah, no worries, mate, just let me know when you want me.' I was sat there half-pissed and I hadn't bought a ticket so I was hardly going to say no (not that I ever would; I'd do the same at any fixture I was at).

The half-time break came and it was time for me to do my bit. The announcer on the Tannoy said: 'St Helens number seven Sean Long is here to make today's draw.' The crowd gave me a round of applause and I was buzzing as I walked onto the pitch to shake hands with the guy with the mic. Next to me was the home team's mascot, Captain Thunder, a big caped superhero with huge rubber abs and biceps. I was stood there, trying my best to be cool while dying for a piss, when Captain Thunder started stroking my head and touching me up. I prodded him back and looked over to where my mates were sat. They were nudging each other and laughing. I think they'd predicted what was coming.

When Captain Thunder slapped me across the face for the umpteenth time, almost knocking me clean over, the bloke with the mic chuckled and announced to the baying crowd: 'Looks like Sean's got his hands full with Captain Thunder.' Next thing I knew, the mad mascot was spanking my arse and I looked back over at the lads and they were killing themselves laughing. Then the mic guy continued his commentary: 'Captain Thunder's frisky today – what do you think of our mascot, Sean?' I said to myself: 'Captain Thunder's cruising for a fucking bruising, that's what I think.'

The mascot finally stopped harassing me when the announcer bloke said it was time for the draw. I put my hands behind my back while I waited for him to sort the ticket machine out and Captain Thunder copied my every move, making fun of me. The lads were still laughing, taking the piss, and I seized the opportunity to get the bugger back. Captain Thunder was looking straight at the crowd and because he had his big fake head on, he couldn't see to his side. So I twatted the cheeky fucker in the stomach and he hit the deck. The crowd went mad and everyone was laughing, especially my mates, who were in raptures. The guy with the mic didn't see me punch the mascot and when he saw him rolling around on the floor, clutching his belly, he said: 'I don't know what's up with Captain Thunder. What's he up to now, Sean?' The crowd of 2,000 were beside themselves; the entire place was in stitches.

Anyway, back to the tunnel in Gateshead in 2009, and bumping into Captain Thunder after all those years. I said to him: 'God, yeah, I remember you. I punched you in the stomach, didn't I?' He replied: 'You did, yeah. You wanker!' We both had a laugh and a joke about it, but I reckon if Captain Thunder had had his mates with him, I might have got my arse kicked that day.

Now rewind back to 2000, the year I was voted the Super League's Man of Steel, an honour that's up there with the Lance Todd. I was only the second Saints player to win it since George Nicholls way back in 1978 and I was made up. It was between Tommy and me and, to be honest, I think he was the better player that year and he should have got it. But the previous year, everyone had been tipping me to win it and I didn't (it went to Castleford forward Adrian Vowles) so I wasn't complaining. And anyway, Tommy was named Players' Player of the Year so I think he was happy enough. I'd picked up that award in 1999 and I think in many ways it's a higher accolade. It is chosen by your rugby-playing peers – including the opposition you battle against all year – and it's a true honour.

Having picked up the two coveted individual player awards and after the drama against Bradford, we were brimming with confidence going into the semi-final eliminator with table-topping Wigan. We absolutely demolished them 54-16 in front of a record crowd of over 19,000 at the JJB. I don't know if it was the talking to I'd got off Basil for jumping into bed with him or my hell-bent desire to beat my old club, but I played out of my skin that game. I knocked over nine out of my 10 attempts at goal and scored two tries. It was a massacre – we were now through to the Grand Final and the Warriors would have to play a final eliminator against the Bulls.

Wigan overcame the huge dent we'd done to their confidence to beat Bradford and fix up a return date with us. But it must have taken a lot out of Andy Farrell's crew because we ran out comfortable 29-16 winners to secure back-to-back Grand Final wins.

We were now becoming the dominant force in the Super League era and I was looking forward to another cushty season in 2001. I wanted a third straight Grand Final and had my eye on a first Challenge Cup win. I've already talked about that first Challenge Cup and my Lance Todd Trophy, but after that I again picked up a shocker of a knee injury when I was late-challenged by Huddersfield's Brandon Costin. It meant another op and a lengthy rehabilitation. And mine wasn't the only injury blow to hit the squad as Tommy, Paul Newlove and David Fairleigh all missed chunks of the season. I could only watch as Saints crashed out 44-10 to Wigan in the final eliminator, ending a season of anti-climax.

On paper, I was fully fit coming into the 2002 season. However, having just recovered from my second cruciate injury, I didn't want to rush things and it took me some time to find my feet. But with the rest of the team playing well, Basil could afford to ease me back into things. This was also Martin Gleeson's first season at the club. Glees and I soon bonded, became great mates and shared some crazy adventures. But it was a bit of a stop-start year. We lost the Challenge Cup final against Wigan and then an injured wrist put me out for another three months. In fact, I went a bit crazy in 2002, but you can read all about that messy year in the next chapter.

Anyway, after the depressing Wigan defeat, Basil let us have a few days off and so me and fellow Saint Darren 'Alby' Albert decided to go for a long weekend in Magaluf – a Spanish party resort with such a good reputation for fun times that it's nicknamed 'Shagaluf'. Bring it on! I recruited my old pals Owen and Poydy to come along, though they took a bit of persuading. Poydy couldn't get the time off work, but after some cajoling he agreed to pack his suitcase anyway and deal with his boss when he got back. Owen was meant to be going on a romantic weekend away to Devon with his girlfriend, but I said: 'Fuck Devon, come to Spain with me.' He rang his girlfriend and broke the news. He was ashen-faced when he got off the phone but, like Poydy, he'd handle the fallout on his return.

We arrived in Magaluf on the Friday and immediately

hit the bars. We were getting smashed in one boozer when Alby clocked a tattoo parlour over the road that advertised cheap piercings. He already had his nipple and tongue done and announced: 'I'm going to get another one.' I went: 'Where?' And he proudly declared: 'My cock!' He asked us to go along with him and I didn't take much convincing. 'I'll do it,' I said. Owen was shaking his head and insisted: 'I'm not fucking doing it, I'm in enough trouble at home – not a bloody prayer.' We pestered him and he relented a bit. 'Okay, I'll get my eyebrow done, but that's it.' Poydy was having none of it, but he came along for the craic.

We drained our pints and walked to the tattooist's, stopping off for some cans on the way. We got in the shop and there was a little Spanish guy sat there and I went: 'Right mate, how much for three cocks and three eyebrows?' Owen looked at me and said: 'I'm not getting my cock done, I've already told you.' I reassured him, saying: 'Look, I'll go first and prove it doesn't hurt. And don't worry about your missus when we get back, she'll love it. It's meant to heighten the pleasure.' So, the Spanish guy took us through the price list: 'The penis is *thees*, and the eyebrow is *thees*. Is cheap value, no?' It really was cheap. In fact, it was so cheap that if I wasn't drunk I think I'd have been put off. There was no need for bartering over the price and I jumped on the bed, whipped my shorts down and said: 'Make it quick, mate.'

The lads were stood around me, swigging beer, and the Spanish guy was smoking. I remember thinking: 'I'm sure these conditions wouldn't be allowed back home...' The guy sprayed some stuff on my pecker to help numb it. Then he brandished a sharp hook – about the size of a large sea fishing hook – and he threaded it through my Jap's eye. 'Oh, my God,' I thought. 'What the fuck have I got myself into?' I looked up at my mates and they were half-smiling, half-grimacing. But something was going wrong. The Spanish guy was tugging on the hook, trying to get it to come through the banjo string. 'Oh, tough skin,' he said as he manhandled my little fella like a bird wrestling a worm out of the ground. I screamed: 'Fucking hell, get it through mate!' I've got tears in my eyes just writing about it!

The ordeal continued for a few more seconds and then I lost it. I sat up, grabbed the bloke and skimmed him across the room, sending him smashing into a table. I immediately felt bad but he wasn't hurt. 'You are crazy man,' he said as he got to his feet. I said: 'Sorry mate, I'm just a bit freaked out.' Then Owen piped up: 'What's the matter, Longy – are you a man or a mouse?'

I was the one who'd told Owen to get it done, so I steeled myself and let the guy have another go at it. Owen grabbed hold of my ankles and Alby held my arms down. All I needed was a bit of leather between my teeth and it would have looked like I was about to have something amputated without anaesthetic, like in the olden days. It went through fine this time and I just went 'Aaah' with relief. Despite the horrendous experience I'd had, my loyal pal Owen jumped on the bed after me, pulled out his old man and said: 'Right, I'm next – stick one through there, lad.' He was done in seconds, the lucky sod. I wondered whether mine was the first the bloke had ever done and now he was getting better at it. Alby was last up and he didn't even flinch.

He's a hard Aussie bastard is Alby. If he told me he used to fight crocodiles as a baby, I'd believe him.

We got our eyebrows done next and that went without incident. Before we left, the man gave us some instructions on how to care for our newly-pierced privates. He said: 'Salt water baths is good for healing and do not have sex for a while.' As we left, he added: 'And no drinking.' We took his advice on board and promptly walked back across the road and ordered four pints with whisky chasers. Me, Owen and Alby were proudly showing off the bull rings in our swollen knobs and everyone agreed we were mad.

After a couple more drinks, Owen announced he was going in the sea. 'The guy said salt water's good for it,' he slurred as he staggered off. When he came back 20 minutes later, the front of his shorts were red with blood. It's a good job there were no sharks around when he went for his dip.

We went back to our hotel and Owen got himself cleaned up. The bleeding had stopped and we all got changed and headed back out. At the end of the night, Owen and me pulled a couple of fit girls who were more than up for a bit of rumpy pumpy. In fact, they were gagging for it, so we left Alby and Poydy and took the lasses back to our place for a good seeing-to. We had a big room with four single beds and we chose the two that were furthest away from each other and got down to business. We all ended up naked and everything was going well until my old man stood to attention. 'Jesus!' I yelled. The pain was incredible. I was so drunk that I'd forgotten I'd had the piercing done and now I was in agony. I looked over to Owen and could make out in the dark that he was having trouble. 'Owen...I can't do it.' 'Neither can I...' he said. 'I feel like the end of my dick's going to explode!' The girls weren't impressed and they didn't hang around. They quickly got dressed, looked us both up and down as if to say 'you dickheads' and walked out. We spent the rest of the weekend sunbathing and drinking and gave girls a wide berth.

As I recovered from my injured wrist, I could only watch as Saints finished top of the table that year. But I was back and raring to go just before the play-offs. As table-toppers we had a home tie against Bradford, and a win would have sent us straight to Old Trafford for the Grand Final. But the Bulls came out winners in a tight game that ended 26-28. Thankfully, as the league's leading side you get another chance and we took ours with both hands when we brushed aside Wigan 24-8 in the final eliminator. I say brushed, but that doesn't allow for the little altercation I had with their Kiwi prop Craig Smith. I went in to tackle the big man and, leading with the elbow, he hit me square in the throat. I grabbed him, told him he was a dirty c**t and tried to stick the head on him. That was a mistake. There was a scuffle and the next thing I knew I was lying on my back on the deck thinking: 'What the fuck hit me?' Craig and I were both sin-binned but when I came back on I was soon in the mix and helping the team on to another big night in Manchester.

After the game my jaw was killing me and I kept telling the physio it was sore but she didn't seem interested. And that was how I came to play in probably the most famous ever Grand Final with a broken jaw. Having a cracked jaw is not ideal when you're against a team as powerful as the Bulls, but I'd been out too long that season to miss the big game.

We felt that if we could keep it close then their big forwards would run out of steam and we could take it late. But that plan looked to be straight out the window when they scored through Scott Naylor after just three minutes. Despite the dodgy start, we managed to turn an 8-0 deficit into an 8-12 half-time lead. After the break, Bradford hit back with two tries in four minutes. First in was Robbie Paul, and then Michael Withers twisted out of Darren Albert's last-ditch tackle to touch down by the corner flag. Anyone watching would have thought that the game was heading Bradford's way but that didn't allow for the Saints never-say-die spirit.

Back we came – it was 2000 all over again – and after Scully had been hauled down inches short of the line, Kez worked the ball to me and I sent Glees over wide out. I missed the conversion – my first failure of the night – but when I fired over a penalty soon afterwards, the scores were level at 18-18. Before the game, the bookies couldn't pick a favourite and they were proved right.

With a minute to go, the call went up for a drop and Joynty took it in under the posts about 15 metres out. On the fifth tackle we produced the slowest play of the ball you'll ever see. Scully and his dodgy hamstring were on the right and I was on the left. Kez looked at Scully then fired the ball to me. A record 61,138 crowd held its breath as I lined up a last-ditch drop goal attempt with the game all set for extra time. I hit it nice and sweet but with the angle I wasn't sure it had gone over. But with 79 minutes and 10 seconds of the match gone it bloody well had and we'd won 19-18! The Saints fans went crazy while the Bulls end all sat with their head in their hands, looking truly heartbroken. Rugby league fans recently voted that drop goal the best Grand Final moment ever. If Scully hadn't been crocked, I wouldn't have kicked it. So cheers, Scully, I owe you a pint.

After the wild celebrations had died down I finally got round to having my jaw x-rayed and the break was discovered. Sometimes I can't work out whether I have a very high pain threshold or I'm just really numb!

CHAPTER 9
SOZZLED IN SPAIN

We never quite managed the highs of the previous season through 2003. Injuries to Tommy, Kez and Paul Newlove robbed us of three of our best players and despite having one of the strongest squads in the league, it was always going to be tough. Leeds knocked us out of the Challenge Cup in the semis and we only managed to finish fourth in the league before Wigan saw us off in the eliminator semi-final.

But if 2003 was an uneventful year, 2004 was a little more interesting. We had the joy of the Challenge Cup final win over Wigan – another big game I played with a broken jaw! But we were unable to build on the momentum of that game and Wigan avenged that day in Cardiff by again knocking us out in the eliminator semi-final – it was becoming a very nasty habit.

And then came 2005, another one I'd probably rather forget. My mentor Basil was sacked by Saints and Daniel Anderson came in as the new coach. I missed a chunk of the early season with a broken wrist I'd sustained when I fell off my motorbike (though I lied to the physios and said I broke it playing against the Broncos). After that, Terry Newton officially ended my campaign by fracturing my cheek and eye socket with his elbow. We topped the table but it was another trophy-free season – people never seem to care or remember who wins the League Leaders' Shield. Hull had put us out of the Challenge Cup and we went out of Super League in the final eliminator. At least this time we didn't have to suffer at the hands of Wigan – Bradford did the honours on this occasion.

But I'm a glass-half-full kind of guy and I always believe something better is round the corner – and it was. In 2006, we started a three-year Challenge Cup winning run. We won the Grand Final that year, too. Saints that year were the best team I have ever played with. If you can leave two international players (Nick Fozzard and Vinnie Anderson) out of the squad for the Challenge Cup final, you know you've got real strength and depth. We were like Chelsea FC back then; the coach was spoilt for choice.

It was our fifth title in 11 years of summer rugby – our second League and Cup double – and the game was played out in front of a record-breaking Grand Final crowd of 72,582, just short of the Old Trafford capacity. We'd lost four games all season and finished an impressive eight points clear at the top of the table. It was Hull's first appearance in the big game and they froze as we ran out 26-4 winners to cap a memorable season.

The following year, 2007, we were red-hot favourites to do the double again but it didn't quite work out like that. It was another stop-start season for me; I'd played 14 straight and then in a Super League game against Wigan I pulled my calf. But it wasn't the end of the world; I was probably looking at just a couple of weeks out.

I was doing my rehab work one morning when the physio got me in and said he wanted me to do some sprinting. It was early and I'd woken up a bit stiff. I pushed off to sprint 100 metres and as I did so, something went in my calf. It cramped up and felt awful. But it was my own fault; I should have warmed up more. The next day a scan showed an 11cm tear. I missed another eight games and my first back was against Catalans in the Challenge Cup final who we beat 30-8. But in the next Super League game against Harlequins I tore my hamstring and was out for another six weeks.

I returned just in time for the Grand Final. That season it seemed like I only played in Cup finals. I was fit for the eliminator against Leeds, but only just, so Daniel left me out and I'm glad he did because it was a really tough game with some big hits.

If I've got a moan about the play-off structure it's the fact that you can beat a team in what is really a semi-final, and they go and get another chance and you end up playing them again in the final. That's what happened when we fronted up to Leeds. We were up for it but there were a lot of sore bodies out on the park and Leeds were definitely the better team on the night. They were all over us and ran out 33-6 winners. Our usual fast-flowing attacking game was nowhere to be seen that night. It was probably one of the most sickening defeats I've had in my career. I was shell-shocked afterwards.

Without wishing to make excuses – and this might explain why we can win Challenge Cups but struggle in Grand Finals – we spend all summer playing in the dry and then the Grand Final always seems to come round in the middle of an autumn monsoon period and it's like playing with a bar of soap. And at Old Trafford they water the pitch too, even when it's pissing it down. It's what they do in football so no doubt the ground staff think it's what we want, too.

We started 2008 with a pre-season training camp in Wales. Usually, we were treated to somewhere sunny like Dubai or Spain but that year the bosses opted for the Valleys. We stayed at the Vale of Glamorgan Hotel near Cardiff, a lovely place with good training facilities, but it pissed down the whole time so we all had a whinge at our coach Daniel Anderson. To appease us, Daniel said: 'Look, we've not used all of the budget up, so if you win this year's Challenge Cup we'll take you all away for a few days.'

The gaffer's incentive worked because we beat Hull 16-28 in the Challenge Cup Final at Wembley on 30 August. After the game, as we cracked open the bubbly in the dressing room, Daniel said he was taking us all to Madrid once we'd played our last league match of the season against Wigan the following weekend. It was a hard-fought derby clash, and we came from 0-12 down to eventually draw 16-16. We were ready for a nice little holiday in the Spanish capital.

We had the following weekend off, ahead of our semi-final Eliminator against Leeds on September 19, and so we flew out on the Friday morning. When we got to the hotel (the five-star Castilla), Daniel said he wanted the weekend to be a 'chill out not a wipeout' because we had the big Leeds game the following Friday. We had no problem with that and we were happy to get into our shorts and chill out by the hotel pool for the afternoon with a couple of beers. But when we got there, towels in hand, it was shut because it was out of season. Someone said: 'What are we going to do now?' The consensus was: 'Let's just get pissed!'

So we got the Metro to Sol, slap bang in the centre of the city, and the place was bouncing. Daniel was with us for the first few beers and then he headed back to the hotel. Before he left, he said he wanted us back at a reasonable time because we were having a James Graham theme night. James – also known as Jammer – is a 6ft 2in 17-stone prop and he's a tough bugger. He'd been named Man of Steel that year and he was the toast of the team. But as well as being a tough rugby player, Jammer also has the gingerest hair and palest skin in rugby (and possibly the world). He also has a very distinctive fashion sense, always wearing huge boots and never being without a man bag over his shoulder. In short, he's an easy piss-take. The idea was that we'd all dress up as him and the best – or, rather, funniest – lookalike would win a prize.

Once the gaffer had gone, we started playing drinking games, including one where everyone had to name a team in the Premier League. If you couldn't name one, or you repeated one that someone had already said, you had to down half a pint of Sangria. Fifteen jugs later, most of us were well hammered. We went round a few more bars, enjoying the party atmosphere and good weather and getting steadily drunker. We figured we deserved a few hard-earned drinks after a punishing Super League season.

By about five o'clock, everyone was leathered. Wello said: 'Come on, let's go back to the hotel. We don't want to spoil Daniel's night.' We all agreed and we made our way back to get changed into our James Graham outfits. When we got to the hotel, instead of going to get changed, everyone headed straight to the bar for a quick pint. That pint soon became another and by 8pm, the entire team of 20 lads – bar Kez, who's teetotal these days – was shit-faced.

We were all sat around, taking the mick out of each other and generally being silly, when suddenly half the lads – the ones facing the lifts – went silent. The rest of us looked round to see what was going on and then everyone started rolling around in hysterics. There, sober as a judge and not smiling, was Daniel – dressed head to toe as Jammer. He'd painted himself all in white and he'd made some big Jammer-style boots out of cardboard (which he'd also painted). He'd really got down to it and made an effort and we just laughed and laughed.

But Daniel's nothing if not a good sport and he was soon joining in the laughter and sitting with us all for a drink. We stayed in the bar for a few more hours and the next thing I knew, I woke up at 9am wearing all my clothes. Kez – my roommate – had already gone down for breakfast and, after a quick shower, I went to join him and the rest of the lads.

As I walked out of the lift, I spotted our chairman, Eamonn McManus, sitting in the foyer. He clocked me, too, and I went over and sat next to him for a chat. He asked: 'So, Sean, what did you get up to last night?' I replied: 'Oh, nothing much, Eamonn. We had a few quiet ones in Sol in the afternoon, then came back to the hotel for a drink and then off to bed.' He said: 'So, you didn't try out the Madrid nightlife then?' Feeling pleased that I'd had a relatively early night, I answered: 'No, I just stopped here.' It was nice to be able to tell the chairman that I'd been relatively sensible for once.

Next minute, Leon came over, said 'hi' to Eamonn, then turned to me and said: 'Jesus, Longy, how pissed were you in Madrid last night? I see you somehow managed to get home…' I looked at his smiling face and then over to Eamonn, who was grinning too, and thought: 'I should have known it was too good to be fucking true.'

Apparently, we'd jumped in a cab back to Sol at about midnight. Me and Lee 'Gilly' Gilmour had ended up play-wrestling in the streets, which explained why my shirt was ripped when I woke up. I was later told that I'd finally staggered back to the hotel at about 4am, trying to swig from a bottle of beer that still had the top on.

Anyway, after Leon's embarrassing revelation in front of Eamonn, I went for breakfast and at midday we all met in the foyer to plan our day. We went to a nice fish restaurant for a civilised meal and everyone was having a laugh about the previous night. With the best intentions, I started on the orange juice. But before we'd finished the starter, someone ordered a few bottles of white wine and we were all straight back on it. It was back to Sol again where we repeated the previous day's boozing. I don't remember how I got home, but Kez told me the next day that he'd taken a few of us back in a taxi.

For once, I wasn't the last one home. Chris 'Flanno' Flannery was out all night and he ended up trying to get on a sightseeing bus at 7am, asking the driver to take him to our hotel. He was shouting, 'Castilla, Castilla' to the driver, who was trying to explain to him in Spanish that it wasn't that kind of bus, that he was taking tourists around the sights of Madrid. Flanno gave up in the end and rang his wife Renee back in England and said: 'Get on the internet, love, and find out where I'm staying and how I can get the hell there.' She asked him what time it was, and he told her. She said 'Sod off', and put the phone down. But he found his way back eventually.

We flew back the following afternoon and, despite the boozing we'd all done, we played Leeds on the Friday and absolutely smashed them, 38-10. We were on fire and it just goes to show the importance of a team-building bender!

So, we were through to the Grand Final again and Daniel – it was his last game in charge before he decided to head back Down Under – told us we had a great chance to avenge Leeds (who'd got in through the back door again) for the previous season's Grand Final disappointment. After the trouncing a fortnight earlier, we were supremely confident.

This was to be the night when we'd show how rugby should be played – Saints-style. But we woke up on the morning of the game to find it was pissing it down. It rained on and off throughout the day and solidly for two hours before kick-off. Our game plan went out of the window and Leeds played the conditions better than us to run out 24-16 winners. Maybe we'd all gone too long without a beer!

CHAPTER 10

BOOZE, BABES AND MAD MIKE

During my first few years at Saints, I lived in a massive Victorian semi at Hall Lane in Wigan. It was a huge place with enormous rooms, high ceilings and a basement; it was perfect for parties. On New Year's Eve 2001, I decided to throw a big bash and invited all my friends and family over. I was going out with a girl called Jodie at the time and she'd been living with me for about three months. It was a bit of an on-off relationship but I was well into her. She invited her family over, too, and it promised to be a top do. I was looking forward to a positive start to 2002.

I was a bit down back then, having snapped my cruciate for the second time the previous year, and I was in rehab trying to get myself right for the start of the 2002 season. Being out of the game for a long time can be very lonely and depressing. When you're injured, you stop being a proper member of the team. You are largely forgotten about until you're right again.

135

Coaches want players who can play. And when you're talking about cruciate injuries, there's every chance it will not recover properly and your career's over. It was a depressing time.

Anyway, we threw the party and some of Jodie's family were there, as were most of mine. All my mates came along and it ended up a bit messy. After midnight, the shots and the Sambuca came out and a lot of us ended up very drunk. To this day I don't know why, but me and our Karl had a fight. We battered each other – Karl's a big lad – and glasses were smashed, tables went over and several doors were ripped off their hinges. I really lost it with my brother that night. Jodie's family were trying to calm me down and Jodie was mortified. The party went tits-up after that and everyone went home.

I woke up on the couch the next morning a bit bruised and very hungover. I looked around the living room and saw the door hanging at a weird angle and with a hole punched through it. I felt sick with remorse. Tank had driven over the night before and he rang me to ask if I'd pick him up so he could come and get his car. I said: 'Yeah, no worries. I'll set off in a minute.' But before I had chance to get up off the couch, Jodie came in and sat next to be. She looked around at the mess and then at me – another mess – and said: 'Well, we tried, didn't we?' I surveyed the carnage around me, smiled back and said: 'Yeah, we tried.'

I nipped upstairs, brushed my teeth and changed my shirt and then went to pick up Tank. When I got home about half an hour later, Jodie's mum and dad were there. I gave them a sheepish 'Alright', and then went in the kitchen to make a brew. Jodie followed me in and said: 'Well, this is the most amicable break-up I've ever had.' I thought: 'What's she on about?' Then it dawned on me. I remembered thinking it a bit weird earlier when she said that stuff about how we'd 'tried'. I thought she meant we'd tried and failed to host a party. She'd actually meant we'd tried and failed to have a relationship. Her parents were there to help her move out. The drunken fight the night before was obviously too much for her. I'd blown it.

I was devastated. I still had feelings for her and splitting up was the worst thing that could have happened to me at the time. I rang Owen, Tank and Wes and they came over and rallied round me. We ended up going to the pub and I got drunk again. New Year's Day is meant to be a time for positive resolutions. But I went off the rails – and stayed off them for most of 2002.

I hit the drink too hard and people were starting to worry about me. One morning in mid-January, I woke up wearing the clothes I had on the night before. I'd had about three hours' sleep and I was still drunk. I was running late for training so I quickly got dressed and jumped in the car. It was a freezing cold morning and I turned up in a tiny pair of shorts, ankle socks and a vest. I'd got ready with no clue what the weather was like outside. To be honest, I was in such a state I didn't even know what time of year it was.

I got to training and started off doing some weights with Scully, who asked me if I was dressed like that for a bet. A few minutes in, we began messing about and he grabbed my vest and ripped it straight down the middle. After weights, we went outside and my ankle socks looked extra stupid when I put my boots on. And I was still half-cut, reeking of booze and wearing a ripped vest and shorts that would not look out of place on a gay roller-skater in San Francisco. Oh, and it was fucking freezing! We were on the front pitch passing the ball and I was a mess. My coordination was all over the place and when I was passed the ball it kept hitting me in the face. At one point Basil said: 'What the fuck is going on here?'

Basil kind of knew I was going through a bad time and after training he took Kez Cunningham to one side because Kez was my mate, one of my partners in crime. He said to him: 'Tell your fucking mate never to turn up to training like that again.' Kez came over to me before we all went home and told me what the gaffer had said. I was embarrassed and said it wouldn't happen again. Of course, it did happen again – many times. But I hid it better.

At the end of January we went on a pre-season training camp to Marbella in Spain. On the first night, we all went out for a few beers to get to know a couple of lads who had just signed, Aussies Darren Britt and Barry Ward. We all had a good drink to break the ice and a few of us ended up quite drunk. The bosses knew we'd all be having a good drink and they didn't mind that much. They wanted us to enjoy ourselves as long as we trained hard. After all, we had a tough season ahead and a happy squad was a good squad.

The next day, we were on the training camp next to the hotel and our conditioner, Jeff Evans, flogged us half to death. It was red-hot and we were all sweating like crazy. I must have sweated about five pints of lager that afternoon! But I pissed it, really. I'd been injured and I'd been drinking shitloads recently but I was fit. I was in such good shape that at the end of the session, I said to Jeff: 'Fucking hell, Jeff. Is that all you've got? Give us some more!' Kez joined in and taunted him more: 'Yeah, come on Jeff – let's have some proper training.' It was like a red rag to a bull and he ordered us both onto the line and said: 'Up 10, back 10, up 20, back 10.' He had me and Kez up and down the pitch, giving us some proper punishment, while the rest of the lads watched. When I got to the end of the field, I decided to give everyone a laugh by stripping off. So off came the vest, then the shorts and then the undies. I was running around in just my rugby boots, my prawn bouncing up and down. And I wasn't even that pissed!

The Russian football team were staying at our hotel and they were training on the pitch next to ours. They'd earlier proved themselves to be a miserable bunch of bastards and when any of us tried to talk to them they just blanked us. We'd say 'hi' and they'd carry on walking. So, I thought I'd run over and cheer them up. They were practising penalties and I sprinted into the goalmouth, jumped onto the crossbar and started doing chin-ups. But the sight of a mad, bollock-naked Englishman did nothing to raise their spirits. They just stood there without a trace of a smile between them. No wonder the Russkies get such a bad press. I've never known a more humourless bunch. Sensing I wasn't welcome, I ran back over to join Kez and found that Jeff was still taking no prisoners. He ragged us around for another 25 minutes while the others laughed at us. I was worried my todger would get sunburnt!

A few weeks after we got back from Spain, the season started. My injury was sorted but it took me a while to get my confidence back. When you've had a serious injury, you worry it's going to happen again and with each knock, you think: 'Fuck, has it gone again?' My timing was a bit off, too, but after a couple of games I was back in form.

But I was still partying a lot. I'd be out every Friday, Saturday and Sunday and then I'd turn up to training on Monday feeling the worse for wear. I had parties at my house all the time and the neighbours hated me. People I didn't know were at my gaff at all times, getting smashed. I'd be out in Wigan or St Helens or wherever and at the end of the night it was a case of: 'Right, everyone back to my place.' I'd regularly have parties that lasted from after the game on Friday through to the early hours of Monday morning. Often I'd go to bed as the sun was coming up, snatch a quick few hours' kip and then drive to training. Looking back, I can't believe I managed it but weirdly, I was as fit back then, aged 25, as I've ever been.

During those crazy, booze-fuelled days, I was as prolific with the women as George Best. That's not a boast, but I was sleeping with different women all the time during those mad months off the rails. I'd wake up in the morning and there'd be a naked girl next to me in bed and I'd think: 'Did I shag her last night?' I'd be so drunk I couldn't remember, but the fact they had no clothes on suggested I had. I'd end up with different girls most weekends. Sometimes I'd be out and a girl would come over and start talking about our night together and I literally didn't have a clue who she was.

Of course, I never let on and it would be a case of: 'Yeah, I had a great time. Would you like a drink?' If she was fit, I'd angle for another go and if she wasn't, I'd make a polite excuse. All that no-strings sex might sound great and I suppose it was fun at the time, but looking back, I think it was an unsatisfying, and often unhappy, time of my life.

After my drinking sessions, I was often woken up by people still partying downstairs. Glees was often there and I knew when he was because he'd play Bob Dylan's *Hurricane* at full blast to indicate it was time for me to get up and start all over again. That song was our party anthem. 2002 was Glees's first year at Saints and he wasn't a senior player back then so he could get away with it. I think I was a bad influence on him but he enjoyed the ride.

Some Monday mornings, after three nights on the lash, I'd get up for training and walk past a sea of strangers all sleeping off the night before. I once went to go in the shower and there was a bloke comatose in the bath, his hands gripping a half-empty bottle of red wine. Another time, I went into my front room to check the rugby news on Teletext and came across a couple at it doggy-style. The girl looked up at me and said: 'Do you mind?' I just left them to it and went off to training. God, they were messy times.

Every Monday I had two cleaners come round – my nan and granddad! My lovely grandparents, who bought me my first rugby ball and boots when I was seven, were still helping me out when I was a 25-year-old Super League player. But it wasn't just a labour of love; I paid them more than the going rate for their trouble. I'd go off to training and they'd let themselves in and give the shithole a going over. If I'd slept in and didn't have time to get rid of the party stragglers, Nan would act as bouncer. 'Come on, you've got to get up,' she'd tell the drunks strewn around the house. 'We've got to clean.' No one messes with my nan when she's got a broom in her hand!

I'd often arrive at training without any recollection of how I got there. I remember one time, we were having lunch at Knowsley Road and me and Glees were in pieces after a three-day weekend bender involving about 50 pints each and a total of around three hours' kip. We were sat with the boys, who were all annoyingly happy, chipper and healthy, and us two were sweating buckets and shaking like shitting dogs. I was chewing on a mouthful of chicken and pasta, trying not to be sick, when Glees jumped up from his seat with his hand to his mouth and ran to the bog to spew up. It's an ugly part of my nature, but seeing my drinking buddy in such a bad state made me feel much better. As long as there was someone worse than me, I was happy.

Monday mornings were hell but once I'd trained and had a shower, I felt brand new again. It was just as well, really, because we had our Saints Monday Drinking Club on the night. A gang of us – me, Glees, Wello, Barry Ward, Darren Britt, Darren Albert and Kez – went over to The Griffin pub in Wigan for a few beers. But while the rest of them went home after four or five pints, I'd be just getting the taste for it. Me and Glees would always be the last ones left and chances were, we'd end up in Chicago Rock in town until

1am. And likely as not, I'd leave with some random girl on my arm.

When you're boozing to the point of collapse, you wake up the next day never knowing how many drinks you've had. Glees and me would often wonder how many we'd necked the night before, debating whether it was 10, 15 or even 20 pints. We could never remember after about the tenth and so we decided one day to put our drinking stamina to the test. At the time, Glees's granddad, Ernie, owned a pub in Longridge in Preston and he agreed to keep score during a Guinness-drinking session one Saturday. Every time we bought a round, Glees's granddad marked it down. By the end of the night we'd supped 20 pints of Guinness each and you should have seen the state of us. One of the pub regulars recorded us on his mobile phone and he showed me the video a couple of days later. We were sat slumped like tramps; we couldn't even speak. But saying that, we still managed to get in a taxi to Wigan where we had a few large JD and Cokes to round off the evening. I drank like this for nearly a year, treating every weekend like it was my stag do. But I'd like to stress that I always stayed off the booze for at least three days before a game. I was daft but I wasn't stupid and my place in the team was never in danger.

I'd played about nine games that season but I was out of action again after fucking my wrist up in the Challenge Cup final. I was injured for seven weeks after that and because I wasn't playing, I had one less reason to stay out of the pubs. But once my wrist started getting better, I did lots of running and weight training. By the time my wrist was healed, I was in quite good shape, despite all the booze, and I was playing well. I knew I was drinking too much and plenty of people were telling me to calm down but I was thinking: 'I'm playing alright, why stop?' In fact, I was at the peak of my boozing when I had one of the highlights of my career – kicking the winning drop goal in the dying seconds of the Grand Final.

2002 is such a blur that I've had to watch rugby DVDs to find out what the hell happened. It was only after watching the Grand Final DVD that I remembered that I was kicking the goals. I could have sworn it was Scully, because I was just back from injury and not 100 per cent. I rang him up and asked him and he explained that he'd kicked the goals in the semi-final but pulled his hamstring so, although he was able to play in the final, the goal kicks were handed back to me. I have a vivid memory of every other season in my Saints career but the 2002 season is fudged. My mind must have been properly puddled.

As if things weren't crazy enough for me that year, along came nutritionist Mike Sutherland. In 2001, Mike was working for the RFL as nutritionist for the Great Britain team. We'd heard he was good, and so we employed him at St Helens. He was a real character who oozed confidence and he had loads of advice that he said would revolutionise our health and fitness. Of the many tips he gave us, two really stand out.

One day, he gave us all a big speech about how we needed to cut tomatoes out of our diets because the seeds stay in your testicles. When he told us, I couldn't believe no one had said it before. He sounded really plausible and we all bought what he said. I immediately cut the evil tomatoes out of my diet. Fair enough, I was shagging anything that moved at that time and fatherhood was far from my mind, but I wanted to have kids when the right girl came along so I was taking no chances with my nads.

I don't know whether Mike was obsessed with our nether regions, but the other tip I remember also involved our tackle. He gave us all a rousing speech after training one day, telling us that if we were going to have sex before a game, it had to be a top dog performance. He said some sporting professionals, like boxers, 'hold it back' to keep the testosterone in, but he told us to 'let it all out'. I remember thinking at the time: 'Why is our nutritionist bothered about whether we're good in the sack?' But he was the expert and we all swallowed it (if you'll pardon the pun). From then on, we gave it our best with our women when doing it before a game.

In case you're wondering why we were taken in by this mad shit, let me stress that Mike had not only been employed by the RFL but he also told us that while he was working with us, he was also the chief nutritionist with the Olympic GB team. You don't get better credentials than that and we were sold.

After injuring my wrist in the Challenge Cup Final, I had to have it reconstructed and went through a lot of rehab. I spent my time training in the gym with Kez, who was also crocked after breaking his hand. Shortly after the surgery on my wrist, Mike said to Kez and me: 'Do you want some stuff that will make you heal quicker?' Obviously, we were both mad keen: 'Yeah, defo Mike, what is it?' We wanted to get back playing as soon as possible and we'd do anything to achieve that goal, as long as it was above board. He said to me: 'I've got something that will get you back within six weeks and it's all natural, all legal.' It was brilliant news. Ordinarily, my wrist injury would take twice that time to be right so I was up for anything. I was dying to get back on the field and so was Kez.

Kez and me were training separately from the other lads and we spent most mornings in the gym together doing weights. Afterwards, we'd go and see Mike and he gave us both an injection in our shoulders. It stung like fuck and neither of us knew what the hell it was he was injecting into us, but we trusted him and we were confident he knew what he was doing. Super League rugby is a big game but we still felt privileged that we had on our staff a guy who headed the Olympic health team. We trusted every word he said and we took three shots a week of the magic stuff and this carried on for about three weeks. 'I'll have you back in no time,' he told us. We thought he was the best thing since sliced bread.

And he was good. In fact, he was fucking brilliant. After three weeks of Mike's injections, I was the fastest I'd ever been. I was 25 and fit (despite the booze) but this was something else. I'd go for a five-mile run and sprint the last half-mile and think nothing of it. I felt like an Olympic athlete and wished we'd employed Mike earlier. I felt fast, really fast, and I was getting times on the treadmill that I'd be chuffed to get at the peak of match play fitness. When my wrist had healed, I played three or four games but I didn't really get a chance to show my pace. But then we played Bradford at Valley

Parade and I showed just how fast I was. Darren Britt made a bust and hit me on the half way line and passed to me. I hit a gap and went BOOM! I flew past the full-back, as fast as I've ever felt – I was a flying machine. The Bradford lads were all chasing me but I was putting distance between us with every stride. I made it past the line, crashed down and thought: 'What's happening to me? I'm like an Olympic sprinter!'

Kez was back on the team again and just after my speedy game against Bradford, he was randomly tested for drugs. He rang me up one afternoon after getting the results and he was nearly in tears. 'What's up?' I asked him, and he said: 'The Rugby League have just called with my test results and they say I've got testicular cancer. They've found something in my blood that means either I've been taking something illegal or I've got cancer.' I was gutted for him. We both knew he had never taken performance-enhancing drugs in his life. I don't know all the science of it, and please excuse me if I've got it a bit wrong, but it turned out he had in his blood an unusually high amount of a hormone that your bollocks produce when you have testicular cancer. The hormone is called HCG (Human Chorionic Gonadotrophin) and it's used to treat underdeveloped testes in young boys and to increase sperm production in men who have fertility problems. If your body produces a high amount of it naturally, it usually means you have testicular cancer. Understandably, Kez was in pieces and so were all the rest of us at Saints. The poor sod had to break it to his family that he had cancer and he became really depressed.

The RFL did more tests and found traces of a masking

agent in Kez's blood, which is taken by drug cheats who are trying to hide something. HCG is used illegally to produce more testosterone, which bulks up the body, enabling you to recover quicker between matches. It also improves performance and can make players aggressive. Kez was now in the frame for being a cheat who had taken drugs to improve his performance on the pitch. It was an awful accusation but we all knew he was innocent. But being branded a cheat was better than having cancer, so Kez was actually pretty relieved. In fact, he was overjoyed.

There was a hearing and Kez was found guilty of taking a banned substance. But in his defence he said he had never knowingly taken anything illegal and he told the hearing all about the so-called 'natural and legal' stuff that Mike Sutherland had been injecting him with. It was then that everyone looked more closely at Mike.

At around that time, an Australian rugby league magazine called *Big League* ran an article alleging that Mike didn't have the qualifications he said he had. It turned out that not only was he not qualified, he also had nothing to do with the Olympic team like he'd said. He used to go missing for four days at a time and when he came back we'd ask: 'Where have you been, Mike?' And he'd come out with stuff like: 'I've been with the Olympic GB team. I had to fly over to Sweden to work with them.' It turned out that the reason Mike went missing for four days at the time was that he was a bloody FIREMAN and he had to work his shifts. So, when he was telling us he was jetting around Europe with the Olympic team, he was actually putting out fires and rescuing cats from trees up the road in Bolton! He had a keen interest in nutrition and knew a lot about it. But he wasn't formally qualified and he took St Helens, and the RFL for years previously, for a ride. Looking back, it all made sense. Sometimes he came to Knowsley Road looking absolutely knackered; he could barely keep his eyes open. We all thought he was jet-lagged but he'd actually just come off a night shift at the fire station. I have to hand it to Mike, he was by far and away the best bullshitter I have ever met.

There was a huge scandal over Kez's drug taking and Mike was sacked. Kez escaped a ban because the RFL were happy that he was given the drug without his knowledge. It was really embarrassing for the RFL because Mike had been their fitness advisor during the 2001 and 2002 Test series against Australia and New Zealand – Mike was obviously so plausible that no one did any proper checks on him. I know St Helens didn't bother checking his credentials because it was assumed the RFL would have already done all that. In any case, Mike was dismissed after an RFL investigation. In a statement, they said: 'We can confirm that Mr Mike Sutherland was released from his contract after an investigation revealed irregularities relating to his professional qualifications. The RFL has introduced a full reappraisal of its appointment system.'

But while Kez went through the mill, he never breathed a word about the fact that Mike had been injecting me with the same stuff, too. Me and Kez have always been good mates, both at work and socially. He knew I wanted to be kept out of it if possible and he kept quiet about me. Very few people know that I was on HCG – until now, that is! When it came out that

Kez had illegal drugs in his body, we knew straight away that it was the stuff Mike had given us. I remember thinking: 'So that's why I feel so good. That's why I'm so fucking fast.' It didn't make sense that I'd be so fit after injury, and while drinking gallons of booze day in day out. It could easily have been me who was randomly tested that day and not Kez and I'm lucky I didn't have to go though what he did. But at the end of the day, we were both the innocent guinea pigs of Mike Sutherland. They say that if something seems too good to be true, it probably is. And in that case, it definitely was.

CHAPTER 11

CALMING DOWN AND FINDING 'THE ONE'

After the crazy year that was 2002, I went into 2003 knowing that if I didn't calm my wild ways I could well end up sacked and in an early grave. Thankfully, I was about to meet a beautiful blonde chick who would make me see the light.

It was midway through January and I was flying out to our pre-season training camp in Lanzarote. Yeah, it's a hard life! We'd just taken our seats on the plane and somebody burst a blown-up sick bag inches away from my right ear. I turned round to give whoever it was a slap and as I did so I clocked a gorgeous blonde air hostess and thought to myself: 'Come to Papa.'

She and another girl had been charged with looking after the motley Saints crew at the back of the plane. I nudged Glees, who was sat next to me, and gestured over to the blonde. 'I'll have a go at her,' I told him. 'I'll have a bash, there's no harm in trying.' We went through the emergency procedure and while the fit bird pointed to the exits and stuff, I was rehearsing how I'd ask her out once the fasten seatbelts light went off. I decided against walking up to her in front of 30 piss-taking lads and saying: 'Hi there, my name's Sean, fancy going for a drink sometime?' It just wouldn't work. My mates – and I use that word loosely – would have a field day. I could just imagine it; me stood next to her, asking her out, and someone yelling: 'Longy, did you get that rash sorted out?'

I was on the aisle seat with Glees and Scully next to me and when the girl walked past, I asked: 'Excuse me, have you got a pen and paper?' I clocked her name badge – she was called Claire. I said we were playing Blob, the card game, and needed to write the scores down. It's hard to say, 'We're playing Blob' and sound cool at the same time.

She brought the pen and paper over and I gave her the eye to let her know I fancied her. She smiled back and I saw a glimmer of interest in her eyes. It was enough for me and I set about writing her a letter. But before I put pen to paper, I remembered that I have shocking handwriting and it was unlikely to do me any favours. I didn't want her reading it and thinking: 'Why am I being asked out by a seven-year-old?' So I got Scully to write it.

The letter went along the lines of: 'I find you really attractive, it is hard to talk to a girl when there are 30 lads peering down my back ready to take the piss, but if you do want to go out for a drink, here is my phone number. I'm away in Lanzarote, but if you fancy coming out with me, text me and when I get back we can go out for a drink.' And I put '32C', which was my seat number.

Okay, it wasn't Shakespeare, but it was to the point. I handed it to Claire's colleague to pass on to her but I wasn't overly optimistic about my chances. Cabin crew must get that sort of thing all the time, randy passengers asking them out – it must be an occupational hazard.

But she must have been impressed by my neat handwriting because a few minutes later, her friend came over and said: 'Claire's in the back and she wants to have a brew with you.' I got a cheer off a few of the lads and made my way up the aisle. We had a cuppa and a chat and we hit it off straight away. She knew we were the St Helens rugby team sat at the back of the plane but she didn't follow the sport so she had no idea who I was. I was only with her for about 10 minutes but that was enough to know she was something special. She said she'd get in touch when I was back from Lanzarote and I went back to join the lads.

True to her word, Claire texted me the day I got home and I was made up. I took her out the following Friday night for a meal at a swanky restaurant in Manchester called the Living Room. It was great, we just clicked and it felt right and I thought she was absolutely gorgeous. I told her that when I spotted her on the plane, I thought: 'Come to Papa'. She thought it was hilarious, which was a promising sign – if you can make them laugh you're halfway there. We went out again two days later and I was the happiest I'd felt in years.

Meeting Claire was perfect timing. For twelve months, I'd blitzed out on booze and birds. I had some fab times but there was something missing in my life. That something was a steady girlfriend, someone to share my life with. Partying most nights and sleeping with dozens of women was fun. But when the partying is over and everyone's gone home, you want someone to keep you company, to cook with and watch telly with. The young, free and single man's party life is often a lonely one. Throughout those wild days, I longed to settle down with someone and start a family. But I never met anyone I really liked. If Claire hadn't have come along, God knows what would have happened to me.

We'd had our first two dates and I couldn't get enough of her. It sounds corny, but I knew I'd found the love of my life. Sadly, just as I was getting myself all loved up, Claire had to fly to Milwaukee for three weeks with work (she worked for Thomas Cook). Those three weeks seemed like an eternity. I rang her every day while she was away and when she got back we started seeing each other properly. It was full on. I was still living in my old Victorian party house in Hindley and Claire was living in Manchester, but we were with each other as much as possible.

Then, one morning towards the end of March, I woke up at 5.30 and sat bolt upright in bed. I was wide awake, which was very unusual for me. I can sleep for England and I lie in as long as possible before getting up for training. I was on my own at home and there was no way I was getting back to sleep so I got up, went downstairs and watched TV. I thought to myself: 'I wonder if Claire's working this morning?' She worked various flight patterns and I couldn't keep track of when she was flying, but thought I'd just give her a ring on the off-chance. I called her mobile at just after half five, not really expecting her to answer. But she did, straight away. She wasn't working either but she was up and about like me, which was quite a coincidence. I asked why she was up so early.

What came next was a surprise, a fantastic one, but a surprise nonetheless. Claire said: 'I've just done a pregnancy test. I'm pregnant.' She asked me what I thought. What did I think!?! Bloody hell!! Straight away I said: 'I'm made up.' That was putting it mildly! I was thrilled. Obviously, it was really early on in our relationship, but it felt right. Like I said, she was 'The One'. It turned out she got pregnant as soon as she got back from Milwaukee, the first time we'd 'done it'. We were both really chuffed and it felt like fate.

The first thing I did was move out of my party house. I decided that if I was going to live with Claire and bring up a baby, I didn't want to stay in that gaff. There were too many memories of drunken benders and I wanted a fresh start. This was the start of a new chapter in my life; I wasn't the party animal any more, I was Longy the family man.

We bought a place in Orrell, on the outskirts of Wigan, where we still live today. We moved in together in July 2003, about halfway through the pregnancy. We were still in our honeymoon period really and it was sweet, we never argued and it was fantastic. It was perfect how everything turned out.

Olivia was born in the early hours of Friday 21 November 2003. I was by Claire's side as she gave birth and it was quite tough what she went through, but at the end of it we had a beautiful baby girl. I was over the moon. But there were some complications when she was born, she had some mucus on her chest and she wasn't feeding, so we thought we were going to lose her and my mind was racing. It was a hairy time because we didn't know if she was going to pull through. I thought: 'We can't lose her now'. But she was fine in the end, thank goodness.

Olivia arrived on the Friday and I was playing for Great Britain against Australia on the Saturday evening in Huddersfield. But my head was battered; we didn't know at that point if Olivia was going to survive. I didn't know much about babies, but I thought if she is not feeding then she is not going to carry on living, so my head was a mess.

Anyway, I drove to the McAlpine Stadium in Huddersfield for the game and realised I'd forgotten my boots. So, I spoke to Graham Steadman, who was one of the assistant coaches for Great Britain and he said: 'Don't worry I'll get you some boots, the footballers have boots here.' He came back with a pair of boots and they were massive! I've only got small size eight feet and these boots must have been about a size 11. So I was running around in warm-up looking like a bloody clown. I thought, 'I can't play in these' so I rang my mate Owen and asked him to nip to my house for my boots and bring them over to Huddersfield as quick as he could. He and our pal Poydy were coming to watch game anyway and he said: 'No worries.'

I was praying they wouldn't get caught up in traffic getting into Huddersfield. The town's roads could get pretty snarled up, especially on a big match day. But I needn't have worried. As they took the Huddersfield turn off the M62 motorway, a police escort appeared and guided them into the McAlpine stadium. This was all organised by my manager, Phil Clarke. So, my mates were escorted like royalty straight into the ground in Owen's battered Transit van. All so I could get my boots on time!

After Olivia was born, we decided to wait a while before getting married. In December 2004, I went to Dubai for a Rugby Union Sevens tournament that we lost in the final. While I was there, I bought a diamond ring. When I got home I walked up the stairs, got on my knees and kept on walking into the bedroom where I asked Claire to marry me. She cried and said yes.

Of course, one of the great things about getting married is the stag do and I had mine at the end of November 2005, giving me two clear months to recover in time for our January 2006 wedding. My best man Owen arranged it all and refused to tell any of us where we were going. 'Just bring your passports,' he told us. A fire engine and a limo arrived and took all 13 of us to the airport. It was only when we got there that we realised we were off to Sin City itself, Las Vegas.

We were let loose in Vegas for four days and three nights and boy, that trip was messy. We played the casinos and won a bit of money but lost a shitload more. When you are playing big money on the tables in Vegas the booze just keeps coming – the casino bosses want every dollar you've got and more besides. If you're drunk, you're judgment's impaired so you keep chucking your money at the game. We ended up constantly drunk and spent shitloads more than we could afford on gambling.

Even by the old 2002 standards, I drank like crazy that weekend. I've never supped as much booze in such a short period of time. We were pissed as parrots for the entire trip, a trip that involved the usual sly stag do tricks. Owen, the evil sod, got me with a real bastard. We were all sharing, two to a room, and after one monumental bender we went to crash out.

We went back to our room and collapsed on our respective beds. Some hours later, I climbed into bed with Owen – maybe I was missing Claire! Unknown to me, Owen woke up with a mouth like a navvy's jockstrap and reached for the glass of water next to him. He took a little sip and spat it straight out. It was vodka! He'd forgotten that I'd filled the glass with vodka earlier when we had all the lads in our room for drinks. So the sly git decided to get his own back (even though I'd done nothing wrong). He filled another glass with vodka and swapped it with the glass of water next to my bed – all the while yours truly was snoring soundly.

Owen went back to sleep, safe and sound in the knowledge that I'd soon be suffering. I woke up a few hours later with elephants clog-dancing in my head and my tongue superglued to the roof of my mouth. After lying there for a few minutes I saw in the gloom the glass of water I'd sensibly left on the table next to the bed. My gob was as dry as the Nevada desert and I grabbed the glass with a shaking hand, desperate to quench my raging thirst. And, unlike Owen a couple of hours earlier, there was no little sip taken. I glugged down half a pint before realising there was something seriously fucking wrong.

If you've ever swigged down a relatively big measure of straight vodka you'll know it burns like a bastard and it makes your eyes feel like they're bleeding. Chug down a half pint, literally like water, when you've got the head from hell and guts bubbling like a witch's cauldron and you may as well have well have supped cyanide.

The vodka seared down my throat like Agent Orange and as soon as it hit my stomach it made the return journey back up. I've never spewed like it and I was retching non-stop for what seemed like an eternity. When the vomiting finally stopped I collapsed on my bed, sweating cobs and drooling bile. I felt like I was dying but Owen – my best friend since childhood – saw the funny side. In fact, I thought he was going to pop his clogs at one point, he was laughing that much. The bastard!

After the mess of Vegas, I had a month off the ale and, aside from a few drinks over Christmas and New Year, I led a largely teetotal existence. But on the night before the wedding, I went for a few quiet beers with my mates. Needless to say, it didn't end up being quiet at all.

We went out on Wigan Lane, on the outskirts of Wigan. It started off with only about six of us but there was soon a crowd of 20, all getting steadily pissed. I was trying to stay sensible and paced myself. I told myself: 'You're getting married in the morning...don't go mad...don't go mad! Please don't do mad, Longy.' I didn't want to have the beer sweats on my wedding day. I should have stayed at home and played Scrabble.

We went into a pub called The Fox & Goose and my brother Karl turned up with some of his pals. Tank and another mate were playing pool and our Karl had a bet with Carl 'Fitzy' Fitzpatrick, who plays at Salford. Karl wagered that Fitzy wouldn't dare disrupt the game by jumping up on the pool table and doing press-ups. Fitzy's not the type to turn down a challenge and next thing we knew, the balls went flying and he won his bet.

Tank was not amused and hit him over the arse with his pool cue. There was a bit of pushing and shoving and a lot of swearing and then my brother ran in and twatted Tank in the throat. It was a hard punch and Tank could hardly speak at the wedding the next day. Poydy leapt to Tank's defence (he's not as big as his name suggests) and punched our Karl in the eye. A brawl ensued and I was stood out of harm's way, thinking: 'Oh, for fuck's sake, I'm getting married tomorrow and half my guests are braying hell out of each other. This is all I need.' Thankfully, it all calmed down before it got too serious. The lads realised that the night before my wedding was not the best time for being arrested and so they all kissed and made up. So, after a troubled sleep, I woke up without a hangover but full of nerves. Tank and our Karl were both ushers and one of them couldn't speak while the other had a full-on shiner. Thankfully, Claire didn't have a clue what had gone on. At one point she asked me why Karl had a black eye, but I just said: 'It's a long story … I'll tell you later.' I never did, but if she's read this far, she'll know now.

Everything went to plan on the day. Well, I say that, but Claire turned up 25 minutes late. I was stood there at the church – St James's in Orrell – and feeling a bit twitchy. The priest didn't help when he said: 'Where is she? I have never had anyone this late before.' Just as I started thinking I was about to be jilted, she arrived. I might have guessed she'd be late, she's late for everything. She calls it 'fashionably late.'

Once the panic was over and we'd said our 'I dos',

we had a brilliant day. All our families were there and all my old friends. I didn't invite that many rugby lads to the day do, but my best playing pals were there: Wello, Wilko, Scully and my old Saints coach and good mate, Basil.

The full team came to the reception at the Kilhey Court Hotel, a lovely place overlooking a lake on the outskirts of Wigan. Glees was on the top table and he was a drunken mess, wrecked on red wine. He was trying to chat up Claire's sister, but he got nowhere. The party was going really well, we had a Blues Brothers tribute band playing and everyone was having great fun.

Then my Saints team-mate Wilko – a fucking crackpot of a bloke – went up to the DJ and asked him to play the Benny Hill theme tune. You know the one, where the pervy funnyman's running around trying to pinch women's arses. Wilko's asked for it at every bash I've been to with him and it always ends up in carnage. So, the tune came on and everyone started running around shaking the finger and doing the Benny Hill thing. Most of us were quite leathered by then and we were doing somersaults and falling over and diving everywhere. I clocked Basil at one point and he had his head in his hands. He wasn't our coach anymore – Ando was – but he was probably thinking: 'They could lose the entire team through injury here.' Well, it wasn't that bad, but he'd have been right to be concerned.

At the end of the Benny Hill madness, someone yelled: 'PILE ON!' So there we were, 20 or so rugby lads diving on top of each other. I piled on and someone dived on top of me, right on top of my leg and I could feel it go CRACK! I felt a bit of pain but, because I was so pissed, it wasn't too bad. However, as I went to stand up, my leg went really floppy, like jelly. It was my left knee again. I hobbled round for the rest of the night, trying not to make a fuss. The bottle of champagne in my hand helped!

Eventually we went up to bed but there was no consummating the marriage that night; the mixture of booze and a floppy knee put paid to that. In the morning, hungover to death, I realised I'd ripped my trousers from the knee to the crotch and my shoes were missing. But that didn't matter. I was married to my Claire and I was the happiest bloke on earth.

That afternoon, we flew to the Maldives for our honeymoon. My knee was agony but we went all the same and it probably did it some good resting in the sun, chilling out and supping beers. I can honestly say it was the best holiday I've ever had. We went to Royal Island and we were treated like a king and queen for a week. When we got home to Wigan, it was a struggle coming back to reality.

My knee was still bad and so I went to see the physio. I decided against telling him I'd hurt it during a drunken pile-on (physios can be a bit funny about self-inflicted drinking injuries).

Instead, I said I'd slipped getting in the pool on honeymoon. It turned out I'd torn my medial ligament, a Grade 3 tear, so I was out for about four weeks after that. It was pre-season so it wasn't the end of the world. But I blame Wilko for putting Benny Hill on. My knee would have still been intact if it wasn't for him. He's got a lot to answer for has Jon Wilkin.

But, aside from my dodgy knee, my home life with

Claire and our beautiful daughter was going brilliantly. She fell pregnant again quite soon after the wedding and our second daughter, Seini, was born on 8 January 2007. And, of course, I had to wet the baby's head. With Olivia, I celebrated with the Great Britain team – Leon, Scully, Jamie Peacock, Brian Carney, Tez Newton and all my mates came down. When Seini was born, we had a bash in a pub near my house called The Delph. All the St Helens lads came down as well as my schoolmates and we got leathered.

The most recent addition to our family is James, who was born on 22 September 2008. Unlike the first two, we had a scan to find out whether it was a girl or a boy. We wanted to know if we could keep all the pink stuff we'd accumulated for the girls or whether we needed to buy blue. We were buzzing when we found out we were having a boy. I think Claire was happy for me, knowing how great it would be for me to take my little lad to Saturday football or rugby on a Sunday, like my dad did with me.

Having James completed our family. I think he is more likely to be a rugby player than a footballer as he's quite a chunky baby. I'd love it if he got into rugby, or any sport really. I think being sporty keeps you off the streets and on the straight and narrow. You make great mates playing a team sport and it makes you disciplined. If he can make a living playing rugby or football I'll be chuffed to bits. But I'll support him whatever he wants to do. He can be a ballet dancer for all I care as long as he's happy. The same applies to my girls.

My kids are my life now. I do everything with them. Before, I was always missing something but now I'm married with a family I feel like I'm the complete Sean Long. Yes, the boozing, the clubbing and chasing birds was fun but all that was nothing to my life now. It's perfect these days. I spend all my spare time with Claire and my kids.

If I get the chance to go for a game of golf with my mates and maybe a couple of jars after, then that's great. But my wife and kids come first.

CHAPTER 12

THAT BRADFORD BET

In 2004, I was at the centre of the biggest scandal ever to hit my sport. Here's the sorry – and sometimes funny – story...

It was Thursday April 8, and the Saints team were in the dressing room at Knowsley Road for a strategy chat with Basil. We'd played nine games so far that season and won them all, including a 30-10 trouncing of Bradford on their own turf. We were on top form. But we had a hectic week ahead, playing Wigan at home on Good Friday, then away at Bradford on Easter Monday and Salford at home on the following Friday. Basil thought three games in eight days was a big ask and said he was happy if we came away from them all with four points.

He told us he was fielding a full squad for the Wigan game to get two points out of them. Then on the Monday, when we played Bradford, he wanted to field a weaker side to keep the lads fresh for the Salford tie four days later. He decided that out of the three games in eight days, he'd be happy if we could win two. He'd made his mind up before we'd played Wigan that he was going to forfeit the game against Bradford.

The Wigan game was really tough. It was pissing it down, evenly matched and bloody hard work. We'd lost all four derby matches the previous season and we were determined to end our jinx. We looked to have done it, too, when we scored three tries in 15 minutes to lead 14-2 midway through the first half. But Wigan had the wind and rain on their backs in the second half and were in the lead as the end came close until I drew the game with a drop goal in the last minute (having earlier missed two conversion attempts). It was a hard, scrappy game and neither team deserved to lose. We all walked off the pitch battered and bruised, thanks largely to a mass brawl in the second half. The following day, I walked into the training room and the lads were aching but quite upbeat.

We were all sat round taking the piss out of each other when Basil came in to talk about the team he had planned for the Bradford game. It's a good job we were all sat down because when he announced the team, I, for one, came close to fainting. Out of the squad he was sending to Bradford, only two players – Wilko and Glees – were from the first team. The rest was made up of 10 reserves, including five debutants. When the team sheet was formally announced later, Basil said our top players were out through injury. But that's not true. I was out with a dead leg but that was it; everyone else was fit to play. He left out 11 senior players who were perfectly fine. They included skipper

Scully and our fellow Great Britain players Wello, Kez and Gilly.

On a level playing field, we were closely matched with Bradford; they had a good team and beating them away with a full squad was no mean feat. Being without three or four first team players would have made the Bulls red-hot favourites. To lose the entire first team squad bar two was a fucking joke. There was no way in hell we were going to beat Bradford at Bradford fielding a team of kids with 11 key players missing. Even if they tried their hardest, even if they put in the best performances of their careers, we still wouldn't beat the Bulls on their home turf. They were too good and they needed respect. You might as well send my old junior team St Jude's Under-11s up the M62 to play them. It was lambs to the slaughter either way. But Basil was the gaffer and it was up to him – it wasn't for us to tell him he was making a big mistake. It was his tactic to throw the game and have the best players rested to play Salford. Basil's a lovely bloke, a real people person, and I have a lot of respect for him both as a coach and a mate. But his tactics that time were a joke. We were going to get pummelled on Easter Monday and I, in common with the rest of the lads, was embarrassed at the prospect. We knew Salford weren't a problem, we'd beat them with a tired squad every day of the week. But you know what they say, every cloud…

Nobody could have predicted Basil's choice of squad against Bradford, including the bookies, and there was money to be made on that game. Me and Glees got our heads together and decided to have a bet on Bradford to win. We left training and spent the Saturday afternoon driving round Billinge looking for a bookmaker that had the handicaps up for the game. We were desperate to get a bet on before news of the team sheet got out and we drove round six or seven bookies. But none of them had the handicaps ready. We could have had a bet on an outright win for Bradford, but the odds would have been crap.

The following afternoon (Easter Sunday) a very excited Glees rang me up to say he'd got the bet on Saints to lose to Bradford by at least nine points. The bookies favoured Bradford because they were at home. They weren't aware they were facing a bunch of trainees. If they'd been in the know, they'd have been offering a much bigger start than nine points. The odds were 10/11 and Glees had stuck a grand on to win £1,909, including the stake. He'd set up a telephone account with the bookmaker Stan James. 'They're based in Guernsey or Jersey or whatever,' Glees said. 'So we'll never get done if we bet with them.' 'Sweet,' I replied. 'I'll ring them now.'

And so I did, the bright spark that I am. I rang up Stan James – who are actually based in Gibraltar – and opened an account with my full name, address and bank details. Like Glees, I wagered £1,000 to win £909. It was the easiest money I'd ever make because the Saints were going to lose by a lot more than nine points. It was a cert. If we had any brains, we'd have put it on a spread bet where you punt per point and we'd have made more money. Of course, if we had any brains we wouldn't have opened telephone accounts to place bets against our own team. But we didn't think that far – we just wanted to make a quick buck.

THAT BRADFORD BET

Me and Glees weren't the only Saints players to back Bradford – far from it. But the others put their bets on with cash at traditional betting shops. The extra-careful ones got mates to stick the money on for them. Apparently, all the bookies had the handicap posted up by Sunday afternoon and the other lads had got on then. Even Bradford got wind of the crap side Basil was putting out and loads of them were on it, too. I heard later that a professional gambler from Liverpool put £50,000 on it. Even my mate Paul 'Scully' Sculthorpe, the Mr Clean of rugby league, wanted to get in on the act. At the time, I lived a few doors down from Scully and on the Sunday evening he stopped by and asked me: 'Have you got on it yet, you got a bet on? Everyone seems to be on it.' I told him I'd wagered a grand with the telephone bookies and he said: 'Do me a favour, Longy, and stick £500 on for me.' I explained I'd already staked a grand and couldn't put any more on. 'You open an account and stick your money on,' I told him. He didn't and I think that's because he's got a brain.

Everyone seemed to have money on Bradford. Players, mates of players, the bloke who sells the pies, the bloke who sells the pies' milkman, the milkman's postman, the postman's mistress and the bloke who collects the mistress's Pools money. No wonder all the bookmakers smelled a rat and closed the book by Monday morning. They stood to lose a bloody fortune.

The next day, we all went in the coach to the Grattan Stadium. Even though we weren't playing, Scully and me went along to watch the game; a game we all knew was about as equally-matched as a fight between Mike

169

Tyson and Jimmy Krankie. Me and Scully were sat at the front and when we arrived at Bradford, Eddie Hemmings – the rugby league anchorman for Sky Sports – popped his head up, and asked me: 'How you doing, Longy? You not playing?' I said 'No'. Then he turned to Scully: 'Scully, are you playing?' Scully shook his head and then Eddie asked: 'Who else isn't playing?' Now, I'm not suggesting he was having a bet, but when has Eddie Hemmings ever gone onto a team coach and asked who's not playing? I thought to myself: 'He's had a fucking bet.' I was putting two and two together and I might be wrong. Perhaps he'd heard rumours of the team sheet and was just checking it was true. But it seemed really odd at the time.

The game started much better than any of us imagined when Glees scored the first try and we went 4-0 up. After that, though, it was a whitewash and they fucking battered us in front of 15,000 fans and a live television audience. We were thrashed 54-8. The kids played as hard as they could and we all respected them for it but they were on a hiding to nothing. They didn't stand a chance. After the game, Bradford coach Brain Noble was quick to take the piss, telling journalists: 'I felt for the Saints fans who had paid good money to get over here. We had prepared to play George Foreman and got George Formby.' It should have been a tight contest between two proud, long-standing rivals. God, it was humiliating.

I was gutted we lost so badly against Bradford and the mood going home was down to say the least. The young lads had tried their best and were just quiet. They'd been pummelled. When I got in that night I thought little of the bet. I'd won close to a grand and we'd beaten the bookies, but I was more bothered about how badly we were stuffed and frustrated at the team we'd sent out. The game was out of my hands because I wasn't playing and, even if I was, the team Basil put out was so weak I wouldn't have made much of a difference. Of course, Glees had had a bet and he'd played, but he gave it his all. I know for a fact that he would have sacrificed his thousand quid (and more) for St Helens to win that game. And so it was that we all went home that night, a bit pissed off but a few bob better off. I never imagined for a second the shit that was about to hit the fan.

Three days after the Bradford game, I was at home watching *Columbo* on daytime telly when I heard a knock on the door. I looked through the window and there was a shifty-looking guy in a suit stood by the front door. When I opened the door, he jumped away to his left, and I thought: 'Who's this dick?' Then I heard a load of clicking sounds coming from the street and I clocked a bloke sat in a car with a camera sticking out of the window, taking my picture. As I tried to take in what was going on, the suited guy stepped a bit closer (though not within arm's length, I hasten to add) and said: 'I heard you placed a bet with Stan James on your own team to lose against Bradford on Monday.' My mind went blank and I could hear only three words in my head: 'Fuck, fuck, fuck!' Then the guy – who said he was a reporter for the *Daily Mail* – asked: 'Did you bet against your own team?' I was not prepared for this and just said the first thing that came to me: 'Yeah, I put it on for my mate.' He noted down what I said then said: 'Oh, you live in a big house, don't you? This is a nice big house.' He was implying that I'd made all my money on illicit gambling, that I'd bought my house with the proceeds.

Trying to sound cool and calm (but feeling like a kid who'd just been caught nicking sweets from a shop), I added: 'The bet wasn't for me, I opened the account for my mate. He didn't have the money in his account so I just said I'd put the money on for him and, obviously, he would give me the money if he lost and I would give him the money if he won.' As he wrote it all down, I thought: 'Jesus, how dodgy does that sound? That's never going to work. I'm well and truly in the shit here.'

As if reading my mind, the reporter asked me if I thought placing a wager against my own side looked 'dodgy'. I agreed that it did but stressed again that it was for a mate. He seemed happy to leave it at that and started to walk back up the drive. But before I shut the door, I called after him and asked how he found out about the bet. 'Oh, someone at Stan James called us up.' Then I wondered: 'Why did my bet ring alarm bells at Stan James?' Maybe they checked through all the bets made on that game after the betting was suspended, looking for people who might have had insider knowledge. Or perhaps the bloke I spoke to on the phone was a rugby league fan and he recognised my name. I don't suppose I'll ever know but I reckon someone at the bookies got a nice back-hander for grassing me up to the press. I'm certain of one thing – me and Glees should have done what everyone else did and paid for our bets in cash across the counter on the high street.

As I watched the reporter and photographer drive off along my road, I had a nasty feeling that all this was going to get worse. A lot worse. I didn't really think what I'd done was bad. Like many other people who had bet on that game, me and Glees had simply bashed the bookies. We got one over on them because we knew our team was weak before they did. It's not like we'd thrown the game or anything (though Basil clearly had by leaving out 11 senior players). But I knew what the papers were like and the moral high ground they always took. The Kieren Fallon horse race fixing scandal was raging at the time and I knew they'd have a field day with this story.

The minute the pair from the *Mail* had gone, I got straight on the phone to Glees, who was at his mum's house. 'The fucking reporters have been to my house,' I told him. I would have put money on his response that was, predictably, 'Oh, fuck!' I said to him: 'They're onto us, we're busted. Look Glees, they'll definitely be coming to your house. Stay away from the windows and don't answer your door.' I was bricking it but, to be honest, I was more excited than anything else. I'd gone from being bored on a run-of-the-mill Thursday to feeling like I was in the middle of a Hollywood thriller.

Ten minutes later, the phone rang. It was Glees. 'They're here! They're here!' he exclaimed. He didn't answer the door and was speaking from his kitchen, blinds closed. I could hear his doorbell go and we were both laughing like a couple of kids. It was a game of cat and mouse at the Gleeson household, only the cat was a weedy journalist and the mouse was a 15-stone nutter, known as one of the toughest blokes in rugby league.

He said he'd sit tight and wait for the reporter to go. I told him about the bollocks I came out with about putting the bet on for a mate and we both agreed it was probably best if Glees didn't make any comment. I hung up and rang Basil to give him heads up on what was going on.

'Basil, it's Longy,' I said. 'Are you sat down?' I told him me and Glees had put a bet on at the weekend on Bradford to beat us. He told me not to worry about it, saying it was not a big deal. He was probably wondering why I was even bothering to tell him until I slipped in the fact that we'd done it in our own names at an offshore bookies and that reporters from the *Daily Mail* were onto the story. Basil went silent for a bit, then sighed 'Ah, mate…' in his Aussie accent. He didn't blow his top or anything and instead stayed really calm and collected. He said: 'Don't come to the game tomorrow or anywhere near the club until we find out what's gong on. Tell Glees to do the same. The media will be all over this.'

Once I'd got off the phone to Basil, I rang Glees back. 'Have they gone?' I asked him. 'I think so, yeah,' he replied, half-whispering in case the reporter was still outside and had superhero hearing. I explained what Basil had said and told him to sit tight and wait for me to pick him up. I got into my wife's car – a little Fiat Punto – and charged round to his mum's house, which was about a mile away. Glees came to the door when I pulled up and I said to him: 'Right, we're fucking off, we've got to get away.' He ran to the car and we sped off. We were halfway up the street when a bloke jumped out with a camera. It was the guy who was sat in the car

Top: Here's me celebrating with fans in 2000 – but I'm buggered if I remember which game it was!

Middle: My dying-seconds drop goal to beat Bradford 19-18 in the 2002 Grand Final. One of my career highlights.

Left: (l-r) Scully, me, Wilko, Edmo and Gardsy at my house in 2004 before heading off to a Saints fancy dress night.

Above left: Me and Glees celebrating our win against Huddersfield in the 2004 Challenge Cup semi-final, just before we were banned for THAT Bradford bet.

Above right: With Saints coach Basil and my baby Olivia after winning the 2004 Challenge Cup.

Below left: Here, I'm talking to the doctor after my pal Tez Newton smashed my cheek and eye socket with his elbow in 2005.

Below right: Me looking like a Viking in 2005.

Above: With the Saints and Great Britain lads after beating the Kiwis Knowsley Road in 2006.

Below: It's celebration time after kicking a winning drop-goal at home Warrington in 2007.

Above: Kez, me and Leon having a bevy to celebrate our 2007 Challenge Cup final win against Catalan.

Below left: Me and my gorgeous wife Claire after I won my third Lance Todd trophy in the 2006 Challenge Cup final against Huddersfield. After this snap was taken, Claire let me loose to get smashed with the lads.

Below right: Francis Meli and me having a dance in the mud at home against Leeds in 2008.

, my third Lance Todd trophy in hand, having champagne poured over head by my Saints pal Maurie.

Above left: Thumbs up to our fans after beating arch rivals Hull KR in our first derby of 2010.

Above right: Taking on the KR defence at the same game.

Left: A pat on the back for my teammate Sammy after overcoming a 20-point deficit to beat St Helens, making it two league wins out of two against my old club.

ove: *(L–R)* Flanno, Matt (Eids), Wilko, Jammer, Robes, Wello, Bryn
a Mad Dog) and me (with a face like a dropped pie).

ow: Me and Nick (my co-author) having a pint.

Above: My new wife Claire and me on honeymoon in the Maldives. She saved me from being the next George Best.

Below: My lovely kids, Seini, Olivia and James – my proudest achievemen

outside my house an hour earlier. I handbrake-turned and put my foot down. It was like something out of *Starsky and Hutch*! We were out of there before they had a chance to follow and we ended up driving aimlessly round Wigan, working out what to do. After about an hour we went back to my house and played pool while trying to formulate some kind of plan. In the end, we decided to wait and see what happened tomorrow and go from there. Glees stayed at mine for a few more hours until we were sure the newspaper guys had given up and then I took him home.

The following morning, the story was splashed all over the front and back pages of the *Daily Mail*. The headline said: STAR BACKED HIS TEAM TO LOSE and underneath there was a picture of me stood at my front door. I located my mobile to ring Basil and found I had about 50 missed calls. 'The press are all over Knowsley Road,' Basil told me. 'I want you and Glees to go away for a while.' I knew Scully had a caravan so I rang him up and asked if me and Glees could hide there for few days. 'Yeah, yeah, no worries,' he said. 'Just get yourself away from it all.' Scully's unflappable, yet he sounded quite shook-up by everything – and he wasn't even involved! This shit really was serious. By 9am, there were newspaper reporters and photographers outside my house. There were even BBC and ITV camera crews there. I called Glees and told him I'd be collecting him and his missus Sam to bugger off to Blackpool. So Claire and I packed some bags, got our little girl Olivia ready and drove past the news teams and over to get Glees.

We raced over to Blackpool, constantly checking behind us to make sure we weren't being followed. We had Radio 5 Live on in the car and our betting scandal was big news. It was all a bit of a buzz but we were meant to be getting away from it all so we stuck in a CD instead. We were at the caravan site by lunchtime and we all chilled out for the afternoon. My phone was ringing like crazy but I just ignored it.

The caravan was on a complex with a clubhouse. On the night, Glees and me went over there for a couple of pints and to watch the game. Of the 11 players out through 'injury' for the Bradford game, 10 were back to play Salford. I was the only one still injured but, of course, I was the only one really injured in the first place. We found a nice spot near the telly and sat down with our pints to watch the Friday-night match. But before we'd had a chance to get settled, we clocked a bunch of lads in Castleford shirts sat a few tables away. We both quickly got our heads down but it was too late, they'd recognised us. 'Alreet, lads!' one of them said. I thought: 'Here we fucking go, they're going to have our lives here.' They came over and we exchanged a few 'alreets' but nothing was mentioned of what was going on with the betting thing. Either they didn't know or they were too polite to say anything. Or, being Castleford fans, maybe they'd seen the article in the *Daily Mail* but weren't able to read it!

The attendance for the game was low, just 7,649. Some of the papers later said the crowd was low because fans were pissed off about the betting, and maybe that was the case. But it wasn't a big game anyway and from the Saints fans reactions I've had, it wasn't a big deal to the vast majority of them. Anyway, St Helens were on top form. Skipper Scully had recovered well from his so-called 'injury' to lead the charge with a hat-trick in the first half. New lad Carl Forber – making his debut in my position of scrum-half – landed four goals and we went into half-time 28-4 up. The game ended 40-4 and went to show how well we could play with a full squad.

We spent the Friday night in the caravan and the next morning we went out and bought all the papers to see what was being written about us. It was mad – the story was everywhere. After all the media interest the day before, I expected it to be big news. But I didn't think for a minute that the coverage would be so harsh. The *Sun* had the headline KICK 'EM OUT which summed up an interview with former Saints player and coach Alex Murphy. He said that what we had done was 'unbelievable, appalling and diabolical.' He told the paper: 'Those two should really be made an example of and if they are forced out of the game for life they are getting what they deserve.' He then went on to mention how much money we earn and how greedy we were. When I read all that I was really upset. He was talking like we'd thrown the game to make money, when it was blatantly obvious that wasn't the case. But Glees and me had a chat about it and we decided that he was probably just pissed off because when he played rugby it wasn't the lucrative game it is today. There was no Super League in his time and he missed out on the money and the glory. We decided that if he wanted to earn himself a hundred quid or so being a rent-a-quote every time there was a player to slag off, then let him do it. He was the same after the World Cup in 2008 when the lads didn't play that well. You'd think a Saints 'legend' like Murphy would play the whole thing down for the sake of the club – whether he was really 'appalled' or not.

We got home on the Sunday to face the music. Thankfully, the media had given up on the story for the time being and everything was fairly quiet. The only contact I had with the outside world that day was when a couple who lived round the corner came round with a bunch of flowers. They were both in the police – he was quite high up – and I used to see them out jogging now and again and give them a nod. Both Saints fans, they came to the door and told me how badly they thought me and Glees were being treated. They reckoned it was no big deal and that it had all been blown out of proportion. It was really nice to hear it – especially from a couple of coppers – when some people were accusing me of illegal insider betting. They lifted my spirits no end.

Glees and me went back to Knowsley Road on the Tuesday to a barrage of piss-taking from the lads. They all thought it was hilarious that we'd bet on the game in our own names when everyone else was counting their winnings without any flak. But aside from the banter, everyone was really sound about it and not one player gave us a hard time. My mind had been working overtime, imagining that everyone would have a downer on us for bringing the club into disrepute. I couldn't have been more wrong. However, the top brass weren't exactly happy with us.

That night, chairman Eamonn McManus took us for a few pints at a pub just outside of Knutsford called The Bear's Paw. He was angry because we'd given the club a bad name. The Saints had sponsors pull out because of what we'd done and he gave us a bit of a bollocking, making us both aware of the fallout of our stupidity. But once he'd said his piece, he was sound. He said the main goal now was to move on from it all and focus on damage limitation. He said he was going sort us out with solicitors and get us looked after. The main thing, he said, was to postpone the RFL hearing until after we'd played our key games. We had the Challenge Cup semi against Huddersfield on April 25 and if we won that there was the final on May 15. We would both almost certainly get banned for what we did and the priority was to make sure it was after our Challenge Cup campaign. He said he valued us both as players and would stand by us, which was a real lift for us. He's a top bloke, Eamonn. He never minces his words and he can be a hard bastard. But he's fair and doesn't shit on people.

We were given different solicitors, largely because having separate ones meant the whole process would be more drawn out. My solicitor told me it would be a good idea to give my £909 winnings to charity. He said it might look good and get me a lesser punishment. And so I did, but I didn't hold out much hope that it would make any difference. While I was trying to score brownie points by being charitable, the RFL was doing its damnedest to blow my story about putting the bet on for a mate out of the water. They even put an advert in *Rugby Leaguer* and *Rugby League Express* magazines asking for information about me and Glees on the weekend we put the bet on. I can't remember exactly what it said but it was along the lines of: 'Did you see Sean Long and Martin Gleeson behaving suspiciously on the Easter Bank Holiday weekend? If so, ring this number.' I rang up and left a message – a minute-long raspberry!

While our solicitors spent their time delaying the case with various legal technicalities and the RFL were asking people to grass us up, we still had a Super League to win and a Challenge Cup to lift. On 25 April – 13 days after the Bradford game – we were at Warrington playing Huddersfield in the semi-final of the Challenge Cup. It was my first game back after the scandal and there was loads of negative shit coming from the Huddersfield camp. Their chief executive, Ralph Rimmer, had been saying I should be suspended from playing until the hearing, and they weren't happy that I was in the squad. When I stepped out onto the pitch the Huddersfield fans were yelling 'cheating bastard' and the like but stuff like that doesn't bother me. If they were all pissed off that I was playing, it was a compliment. Some players get really put off by that kind of thing but for me, it's the opposite. My job was to piss them off even more by playing out of my skin. I'd had a fortnight off; I was determined to prove my loyalty to the Saints and I wanted to wind up the Giants fans. I ended up playing a blinder and winning my second Lance Todd trophy.

My kicking game was the best it had been all season and every bounce went my way. I was in the zone and loving every minute of it. The 4,000 Giants fans booed me every time I touched the ball but that just increased my energy and focus. We scored eight tries – I got one of them – to win 46-6. It was Huddersfield's first Challenge Cup semi-final for 33 years and we outclassed them.

Our team was at full strength (Glees was back, too) and many pundits said afterwards that it was one of the most one-sided semi-finals since Wigan beat Bradford 71-10 in 1992.

But 20 minutes from the end, I went in for a tackle, Chris Nero lifted his elbow up to me, and he hit me on the chin, right on the button, and I felt something split; I felt like my tooth had come away. But within seconds I knew it was worse than that. I suspected I'd broken my jaw. I was in agony and had to come off and leave Scully to take the kicks, which he did admirably, scoring four goals in four attempts to add to my three.

There was a party back at the club that I wasn't going to miss. I was man of the match and we were through to the Challenge Cup final against the evil Wigan Warriors – piss-ups like that don't come along very often and I wanted to be part of it, bust jaw or no bust jaw. The pints and the champers soon helped dull the pain but I couldn't eat a thing. I tried eating a bit of rice but chewing was torture. I was in a bad way and there was nothing that could be done about it at that moment in time so I got drunk with the lads and buzzed about the upcoming game. It was a repeat of the decider two years earlier that Wigan won 21-12. But we were the in-form team and the bookies had already made us 1-2 favourites to lift the trophy for the fourth time in nine years. I really fancied our chances but I resisted having a bet!

The next day, I went for an x-ray and it confirmed my jaw was broken. But it was a clean break that had stayed in place so it could have been a lot worse. And anyway, there was no way I was missing the final against Wigan.

We were up in front of the RFL in June for the betting debacle and I would more than likely be banned, so my season would be over then anyway. I was willing to risk my jaw to play my part in the final. I decided that when I got banned, I could have a rest then and sort it. The doctors weren't too pleased but it was up to me in the end and I was determined.

May 15 came quickly after two easy wins in the league, including a 56-10 drubbing of Leeds at home. But league matches were nothing to a Challenge Cup final (especially against Wigan) and I went to the Millennium Stadium that day as excited as I've ever been about a game. It turned out to be one of the games of my life and I won my second Lance Todd trophy.

A month later, on 17 June, me and Glees had our hearing at the RFL HQ at Red Hall in Leeds and as we drove into the car park, there were cameras everywhere. We walked into the building, past the press, and had a quick meeting with our briefs before the hearing. We weren't sure what to expect and we guessed that we'd either get a hefty fine or, more likely, a ban. But this was the first case of its kind in rugby league so even our lawyers admitted they were in the dark. All they advised us to do was admit to everything and tell it like it happened. We intended pleading guilty to everything anyway. There was no way we were going to lie at an official RFL hearing and get ourselves tied in knots by some hot-shot barrister.

We admitted using insider information to bet on our team to lose and apologised to the RFL advisory panel for it all. We took the match stats in with us that showed Glees had scored the first try and tried his best, proving there wasn't any match-fixing like some people were saying. We explained that we knew we'd have a weakened team and saw the opportunity to sting the bookies. Andy Farrell, the Great Britain skipper, came along as our character witness and he was a star. He said that in 15 years of top-flight rugby he'd never been told that he wasn't allowed to bet on games. He said loads of players had a punt, just to keep an interest. He did really well for us, did Faz. He said we'd been silly and naïve to bet against our own team but that we weren't cheats.

At the end of the hearing, judge Peter Charlesworth – who tries murderers when he's not on the RFL panel – fined us both £7,500 plus £2,205 costs. If that wasn't bad enough, he banned me from playing for three months and Glees for an extra month because he'd played in the game. We were really pissed off. We were thinking a hefty fine and maybe a month's ban. We had to pay the fines, court costs, our solicitors' fees and do without our wages for the length of the bans. For me, that meant the bet on Bradford cost me close to 50 grand. Our solicitors said it could have been worse but that was small consolation. We went to a pub and drowned our sorrows with a few pints of Guinness.

We went to see Basil the next day and he told us to get away while the heat died down, so we headed down to Newquay for a long weekend with my mates Cat Fish, Dyson and Dan Cotton. After months of uncertainty and worry about what would happen at the hearing, I felt like a huge weight had been lifted off my shoulders. We'd come out quite badly with the fines and the bans, but it was over with now. I felt better than I had in ages.

We stayed in a hostel in Newquay with loads of students who'd just broken up for the holidays and we had a riot. I remember being on the beach one night, sat round a fire with a cold beer in my hand and thinking: 'I should get banned more often!'

Basil told us to stay away from Knowsley Road for six weeks, so after we got back from Newquay, Glees and me trained on our own for five weeks, going to the gym every day. Once the six weeks were over, Glees was sold to Warrington. The scandalous Bradford game ended up being his last for Saints. But I was back in team training and things started to get back to normal. Even though I wasn't being paid during my ban, it was assumed I'd train as usual if I wanted to keep my place in the team. Even if it wasn't expected of me, I'd have gone anyway. I had a chance of being picked for the GB team that year and I needed to be fit. You can't get properly fit training on your own.

My ban expired on 17 September, meaning my comeback game was – wait for it – away at Bradford! I thought Basil was pulling my chain when he told me. I knew that it was going to be a tough game, but Basil rested some players again. It was the last game of the season before the play-offs and we couldn't finish any higher in the Super League, so he fielded a weaker side. Everyone at Saints knew it was going to be a difficult game for me but I had to get a match under my belt before the play-offs. We were playing Wigan the following week and I had to be fit and ready for it.

When the coach pulled up at the Grattan Stadium, I felt nervous but also quite excited. I knew the Bradford fans would be give me loads of shit but hey, I love being the centre of attention! The coach door opened and we walked towards the dressing room. It's a funny layout at the Grattan, and you have to walk under a spectator stand to get to the dressing rooms. As we got to the entrance to the tunnel, I heard a load of Bradford fans yelling at me: 'Long, you fucking cheating c**t.' Next thing I knew, someone threw a bucket of water and it went all over our physio, Claire Mannion! She was soaked through. Obviously, the water was meant for me and I just looked up at them, stuck my thumbs up, and said: 'I hope your team are as on target as you dickheads.' That just sent them mad and they were yelling all kinds of insults at me. But I was laughing my head off. I love that kind of shit and it made me desperate to get on the pitch for more. We ended up getting hammered again, this time 64-24. The Bradford fans booed me every time I got the ball but the Saints fans were great with me.

I was glad when the 2004 season was over. The betting debacle was a bad thing for Super League and I just wanted to close that chapter in my life. And to be fair, I was allowed to do just that. I'd still be known as the idiot who backed my team to lose in my own name, but the St Helens establishment didn't hold it against me. Unfortunately, they weren't quite as forgiving with Basil.

The Chairman and the Board were pissed off with him for deliberately fielding a weakened side for the Bradford game. If it hadn't been for the bet, it wouldn't have been such big news. But as it was, it put the spotlight on St Helens for all the wrong reasons and it was an embarrassment for the club. Me and Glees got the public flogging for the bet, but behind closed doors it was Basil who got it in the neck. I – and many of the other lads at Saints – thought the writing was on the wall for him after that.

And we were right. A few months into the next season, Basil was given the elbow for what we all knew was never a sackable offence. He had a rant at some guy who did the media relations stuff for Saints. He gave him quite a hard time, apparently, and he was effin' and blindin' at a good rate. But that kind of thing happens all the time. If everyone who shouted and swore at other members of staff got sacked, there'd be no one working in rugby. Apparently, Basil had had a few warnings after that but still, it didn't seem right and it's just my opinion, but I reckon they were looking for an excuse to get rid of him. After all, it's not like we had a bad start to the 2005 season. We'd won about 12 games on the bounce. They were dirty with Basil and I've always felt sorry for him. And I still feel pretty fucking guilty about putting that Bradford game in the spotlight.

CHAPTER 13

A LEAGUE OF GENTLEMEN

'I want to make it absolutely clear to everyone that I did not tackle Sean with any intent to cause injury.' That was what my GB team-mate Terry Newton said in a statement to the press after he'd nearly removed my head with a vicious elbow-led forearm smash in a Super League game between Wigan and Saints in September 2005. Jesus, I'd hate to see Tez when he really means to hurt someone.

Tez and me have been mates since we were six. We grew up on the same Wigan streets and we knew all the same people. Even back then, he was a tough bugger who knew how to look after himself. You had to be like that to get by where we're from. When we played together for Great Britain and England we always got on and he was a handy bloke to have on your side. He played rough, tackled hard but he was a nasty bastard with it. It was just his game and it's what makes him one of the best players of his generation.

But something short-circuited in Tez's brain that painful day in 2005 and he totally lost the plot. I still wince at the memory. We were 6-14 up when he had his first moment of madness. He hit Lee Gilmore with his forearm in a head-high tackle that knocked the poor lad out cold. I was there first and I pushed Tez and said: 'You're fucking out of order.' He didn't say anything back to me but I could see it in his eyes that he'd gone; they'd glazed over and he looked like a man possessed. Gilly was playing as a makeshift winger after we'd lost Darren Albert early doors. The last thing we needed was to see him carried off on a stretcher – his neck in a brace – after a dirty foul. But the referee copped out and put Tez on report. To my mind, the 'on report' sanction is one of the most stupid rules in rugby league. Referees are there to make decisions, and sometimes they put a player on report for an offence they've clearly seen, but rather than send him off, they'll just give the penalty and stand there with hands crossed. This was a classic example of a ref failing to do his job. If Tez had walked, I would have been spared a lenthy operation, weeks of pain and months out of the game.

With the first half nearly over I got the ball close to their line and I darted sideways to drop off a little inside ball to Maurie Fa'asavalu. As I'd turned to the right I felt a CRACK and a searing pain all down the left hand side of my face. I slammed into Maurie, who's a big bloke, and I thought: 'Fucking hell, what was that?' It didn't feel like I'd been tackled, it felt more like I'd been hit across the face with a cricket bat. I knew it was bad so I got to my feet and put my hand to my face. My left cheek was all caved in and I was in extreme pain. I wasn't concussed, I knew where I was and what was happening but I didn't have a clue what had hit me. Straight from the following play, we scored a try and as I was stumbling back to the halfway line, the doc came running on and said: 'Are you alright?' I said nothing but he felt my face and answered for me: 'Bloody hell ... no.' He helped me off the pitch. I was in serious pain and the doc got me to swallow some strong painkillers. Once I was on the sidelines I was feeling sick and in a bit of a daze as the drugs kicked in.

As I sat in the changing room with my head in my hands, I looked up and asked: 'What the hell happened out there?' One of the physios answered: 'Terry Newton hit you.' I said: 'What the fuck with, a brick?' They told me he'd come in blindside and smashed my cheekbone with his elbow. Now, I've had more knees and elbows in the head than I care to remember but I've known nothing like that. It was only when I later watched the replay that I realised just how bad Tez's challenge was. It looked like he went in to hit me with his shoulder but then lifted up his elbow at the same time. I can see now that he accidentally caught me with his elbow, but at the time I would have loved to punch the bastard hard in the face. But, of course, if I walked up to Tez and punched him, I doubt I'd be walking away afterwards.

The specialist I needed to see wouldn't be available until the following day so there wasn't much point in going to hospital. The doc said I was better off spending the night in my own bed with plenty of strong painkillers. I got on the coach for a lift home and the mood was quite upbeat. We'd won 12-38, securing us the league leaders' trophy, but it'll always be remembered as the game when

Terry went mental and cleaned out Gilly and me. We'd just set off when my phone rang. I looked at the display and it said 'Tez'. But I wasn't in a fit state to talk to anyone at that moment, let alone Terry Newton, so I didn't answer.

When I got home, Claire rushed over to me. She'd seen the tackle on TV and she said: 'Oh my God, are you alright?' I was in agony so I dosed myself up with more tablets and tried to get some sleep.

The next day I saw the specialist and discovered what I already suspected – my cheek and eye socket had been shattered. Two days later I went in for surgery. Hats off to my surgeon; he did a fabulous job. I've got a small scar under my eye where they went in, but most of the work was done from inside my mouth. It's a bit like repairing a dented car panel because they actually push the bones out and back into shape. I had to have three metal plates inserted to knit the bone back together.

While I was recovering in hospital I read in one of the papers that Tez said he'd apologised to me and I thought: 'How? By telepathy?' He might have *tried* to say sorry when he rang after the game but he never spoke to me. When I was out of hospital I again watched coverage of the game and thought: 'How could you do that to a mate?'

The RFL dealt with it and Tez was fined £600 and banned for 10 matches – three for what he'd done to Gilly and seven for the assassination attempt on me. He then had the nerve to appeal, claiming the punishment was excessive. Thankfully, the RFL board agreed he was taking the piss by appealing and added another couple of games to his ban for good measure.

It ended up being months before I saw Tez again. We were called in for a Great Britain training camp the following season. He saw me, wandered over and said: 'Alright?' I replied: 'Yeah, not too bad' and I could tell he wanted to get something off his chest. And then it all gushed out. 'Honest, honest I meant to do Gilly but I didn't mean to do you.' And that was Tez's way of apologising! But I thought 'fair enough', and that was it done with. I've long since forgiven him. How could I not after that beautiful apology? Despite his hard exterior, Tez is a funny bloke with a sick sense of humour that I love and I buzz off him. We don't see each other very often these days, but when we do we're thick as thieves. I always felt we were out of a similar mould – although Tez is probably even dafter than me. After what happened a lot of people told me I should have sued him, because if he'd done it out on the street he could have gone to prison. But I've always believed that what happens on the field stays on the field.

In my case, what happens on the field all too often ends with me getting crocked. It's a tough game but some players seem to get away really lightly on the injury front while others, like yours truly, spend half their time on the treatment table. I totted it up the other day and I've actually been under the knife 20 times. Here's the roll-call of injuries that have been a feature of my career. One fractured cheekbone, one fractured eyesocket, three broken noses, three broken jaws, too many stitches to count, popped AC joint in my shoulder, biceps ruptured in both arms, one broken arm, one broken and reconstructed wrist, two broken thumbs, two broken fingers, two reconstructed knees, medial ligaments torn off the bone in my left knee, cartilage trimmed and removed in that same knee, floating bone removed from my right ankle, a torn ligament in my right ankle and a partridge in a fucking pear tree!

It's staggering how much the human body can put up with. And the worrying thing for the kids who are just starting out is that I reckon it's getting tougher. It used to take one or two days to recover from a game but now it takes anything up to a week. Often players can't walk the day after playing and as the season goes on everybody plays with injuries, knocks, sore shoulders or tweaked hamstrings. But that's just the way it is and everybody accepts that as a professional sportsman. There are games I've played in when I've taken a knock on the head and I have no memory of the rest of the match.

You've heard of an eye for an eye – well, one of my more serious injuries almost ended up being a knee for a knee. In 2001 I did my cruciate for the second time when I was late tackled by Huddersfield stand-off Brandon Costin – an Australian with a dodgy disciplinary record Down Under. I'd put through a kick on the fifth tackle and the ball was long gone when my foot came back down and was planted firmly on the ground. That was when Costin's ridiculously late tackle took me out and the ligaments went for a burton. It was painful as hell and having had the same injury back in my teenage years at Wigan, I knew my season was over and there could be doubts over me ever playing again. My dad was furious. He told me he was going to find someone to kneecap Costin, and it took a lot of begging from me to persuade my old man that it was not a good idea. Looking back,

I'd like to think Dad wasn't really going to resort to a Mafia-style punishment but at the time he seemed pretty serious about the whole thing. Actually, when you consider Costin picked up just a three-match ban for ending my season, then maybe Dad had a point. Perhaps it's time the rugby league bigwigs took a look at some Bernard Long-style measures to bring wayward players into line!

It was a c**t's trick from Costin but I'm not going to suggest he intended to put me out for months. He probably thought he would knock my confidence for the rest of that game with a naughty hit. In football, you always hear players claiming they would never go out to deliberately hurt another pro. I'm always a bit dubious about that when you look at some of the challenges that go in. And in rugby there always has been – and probably always will be – the players who think they'll hit you out of your stride by giving you a dig. But that's always been part of the game. Even in my junior days at St Jude's there were lads who dished it out – usually the ones who went home crying to their mums if they were ever on the receiving end.

Punch-ups have always been part of rugby. Just like in the school playground when everyone gathers round when a fight kicks off, the crowds love a barney. Back in 1998 (if my battered head remembers correctly) we were playing London Broncos at the Stoop, where we were clear favourites to win. But it was a tough place to go. We were sitting in the dressing room when our Australian prop Brett 'Goldie' Goldspink burst in. He'd been talking to an Aussie mate of his, Luke Goodwin, who played for the Broncos and who Goldie knew from his Oldham days. He wasn't playing in that game and when they were chatting, he'd said: 'Hey Goldie, they're going to upset you boys today. First scrum that goes down they're going to kick off and punch anything in a Saints shirt.'

'Aye-aye' thought Goldie, and he was straight back to the lads to tell us what the opposition had planned. They thought they were going to jump us but, unbeknown to them, we were ready and waiting for them. As we went out to warm up, we were psyching out the opposition and giving them evils. They must have wondered what the hell was going on. Anyway, the game started and right on cue, somebody knocked on and the forwards came in for the first scrum. Before it even packed down we went 'Fuck off!' – Brett smashed their prop Mark Carroll and Scully and Kez were in there scrapping.

I realised I was too small to get involved with the brawling big lads. I turned round and spotted Shaun Edwards, who was the Broncos' scrum-half, and I thought: 'Right, you're fucking having it'. I whacked him in the face and next thing we're rolling around the floor under two packs of forwards. We just blitzed them and I battered Shaun. I thought to myself: 'That's for not passing me the ball back in the Wigan early days, you shitbag!' All part of our wonderful game.

I've been lucky enough to have worked under some of the finest coaches in rugby and hope I've had enough sense to pick up some tips from them all. I've got on with all the coaches at Saints and wouldn't hear a bad word said about any of them. It was Shaun McRae, the Aussie with the porn star 'tache, who saw the talent in me, rescued me from Widnes hell and took me to St Helens. I owe a lot to him. Shaun was great, always cracking jokes. But if there was a down side to his coaching, it was his video presentations where we had to sit for hours reviewing and previewing games. I found it really bloody boring. Shaun's knowledge of the game was immense but sometimes he'd try to pass on just a little too much. He knew everything about every player, which foot they stepped off, how they liked to tackle, when they went for a shit – well, maybe not quite that much, but not far off. There was only one thing that really used to annoy Shaun and that was the rain. He fucking hated it. Sometimes we'd train out the front at Knowsley Road where there's a grass area and if it was raining, he would stand in the souvenir shop out of the wet and watch us from there. After two years in charge he left in 1998, basically because of a lack of trophies, I think. Saints were a club used to winning things and after picking up the Challenge Cup in '97 we struggled and had a poor Super League in '98.

That was when Ellery Hanley arrived. Ellery had an aura about him. As soon as he entered the dressing room there'd be silence; Ellery commanded total respect. When he came to Saints he was new to coaching and quite raw. He'd had a little experience on the coaching staff at Balmain Tigers in Australia, but he'd never been a head coach. At this early stage he wasn't the greatest tactician but he got us doing the basics right and even had us practicing playing the ball, a real basic of the game. He hated people giving away silly penalties, back-chatting to the ref, that kind of thing, so our discipline under Ellery was superb. But his biggest strength was his ability to bring a team together. 'This is our family,' he'd say and nobody messed with the family. We'd do anything for each other and Ellery would do anything for the players.

One story from the '99 season probably best sums up the man. We were playing Leeds at Headingley late in the season on a Friday night. The game was live on Sky with an 8pm kick off. As we travelled along the M62 we were caught up in some nightmare traffic and ended up arriving at the ground with only about 20 minutes to spare. Eddie Hemmings, Sky's presenter, came up to Ellery and said they could delay the kick off by 15 minutes if really necessary but, to everyone's amazement, Ellery said: 'No, don't do that. My players will be ready.' I'm thinking 'What the fuck?' as we're all trying to get strapped up and pull our kit on. But with minutes to go we were ready. Ellery had us all gather round in a huddle and started to run down every player in the team, giving everyone an individual boost. 'Paul Aitchison, my champion full-back. Our last line of defence and the man we can all rely on,' and then, 'Paul Newlove and Kevin Iro, the best centre pairing in the world,' and it went on like that through the whole team. It was really inspiring and we were all pumped up and ready to die for the team as we prepared to run out on the park.

And then skipper Chris Joynt said: 'Freddie, you forgot Freddie'. Ellery had failed to mention Freddie Tuilagi, our Samoan winger. But, Ellery being Ellery, quickly rescued the situation. 'You may think I'd forgotten Freddie Tuilagi,' he boomed, 'but I saved the best to last'. If that had happened to anyone other than

Ellery, it would have had us giggling like schoolboys. But with him, it just inspired us even more. We went out, and with barely a chance to warm up, beat Leeds in their own back yard.

That was Ellery, a real players' coach who, unlike any other I've worked with, never swore. Take the swear words out of most coaches' vocabularies and they'd be bloody mutes! He never really bollocked anyone and he got angry with senior players who gave the youngsters a hard time. If a player dropped the ball and someone had a go at them, Ellery would step in with something like: 'Hey, give the kid a break. He didn't mean to do it.' My good mate and half-back partner Tommy Martyn was pretty old school in that respect and would always be telling the young players to pull their fingers out. He wasn't doing it in a bad way, it was just how Tommy had been brought up in the game but Ellery didn't like it.

We won the Grand Final in '99 under Ellery. But we were hammered 44-6 against Melbourne Storm in the World Club Challenge at the start of the 2000 season and then lost our opening Super League game at home to Bradford. He'd had a few rows with the Saints board since coming to Knowsley Road and the writing was on the wall. But I think Ellery had taken us as far as he could at that time and we needed a new coach to move us on.

His replacement, as I've mentioned before, was Ian 'Basil' Millward. Basil had a very promising junior career as a player, but he was forced to quit with a serious neck injury. He came to Saints via Leigh Centurions, where he'd taken a struggling side facing relegation and turned them into promotion contenders. Basil is probably the cleverest coach I've ever worked with; maybe a little too clever at times. I really got on with Basil, he was like a second father to me. I think he saw of bit of himself in me because I was a Jack-the-lad and always messing about. His coaching was superb. He loved his attacking moves and new plays; sometimes we'd have different moves for different games. At times the only way I could keep all the information on board was by writing the strategy on the strapping on my hands before a game.

He was attack-orientated and his motto was 'if they score 30 we'll score 32', and that was the rugby we played. Our defence wasn't the best but some of the attacking moves he came up with were unbelievable. I matured under Basil in so many ways and he realised that, too. I'd settled down with Claire and calmed down massively after that crazy 12 months of 2002. I was really chuffed when, during the 2003 season, Basil made me captain when Joynty and Scully were both injured.

It really meant a lot to me that Basil felt he could trust me to lead his team. I'd been off the rails but I'd got my life back on track and I think that was a key point in my career. Taking on extra responsibility gave me a confidence boost that really helped my game. But Basil's time at Saints ended in controversy, as you've already read. When he left I was gutted.

His replacement was another Australian, Daniel Anderson, who came to Knowsley Road from Auckland where he'd been coach of NRL side New Zealand Warriors. He organised a meeting with me, Kez and Scully to introduce himself and I admit I was a little bit standoffish at first (if you pardon the pun) because Basil was my mate and Daniel was taking his job.

I had my guard up but soon came to realise what a great coach he was. If Basil's strength had been his attack game then Daniel's was certainly his defence. He was superb and, within weeks, took us from being a bit shoddy on the defensive side to being the best in Super League.

His man management was great, too, and he brought the youngsters into training with the seniors. Early in his time with us, he pulled me to one side and told me how he liked to play his team with his scrum-half running the show – like Stacey Jones had done for him at the Warriors. He looked at me and said: 'Can you run this team for me?' Fuck, yes! I told him I'd take the team where he wanted it to go.

But my new role led to problems on the field, where I was always clashing with our captain. Scully would make a call, I'd disagree with him and we'd be forever banging heads. Daniel had told the team that I was running play but Scully didn't like it. All the lads went with it but I got so pissed off with the situation that I went to Daniel and the chairman and said that I was considering leaving. It might sound like I was spitting my dummy out because I wasn't getting my own way. But it wasn't that. I love my rugby but I need to enjoy it to play well. It had got a point where I wasn't enjoying it and that was bad for me and for the team.

There were a few Australian clubs sniffing round but Saints wanted to keep me. Daniel said he'd sort everything out and, true to his word, he did. I don't know what he said to Scully but the arguing stopped and we concentrated on becoming the best side in Super League.

I was vice-captain so when Scully was injured, I stood in. I'd done that since Basil first gave me the opportunity to lead the side back in 2003. And in 2006 it meant I had the chance to pick up a major cup as captain, the only time that's happened in my career. It was a wonderful buzz when I led the team to receive the Grand Final trophy after we'd beaten Hull.

The following year, I started 13 games as captain. When I was injured and spent six weeks out of the game, my old mate Kez took over the captaincy. But in my first game back, I was walking down the tunnel to toss-up when Daniel said from behind me: 'You're not captain, Keiron is.' I looked at Kez and he just shrugged and that was it. I was pretty pissed off, not because I minded Kez doing the job – he was really good at it – but because I'd have expected a bit more tact from Daniel. If he'd sat me down and said he wanted Kez to continue, I'd have said: 'Sweet, no problem.' I was annoyed at being put in such an embarrassing position.

To be honest, I've never wanted to be captain on a permanent basis. I can't be arsed with all the functions you have to attend and all the hands you have to shake in formal situations. And, of course, I like to have beers with the boys when I go to a rugby bash. You can't do that if you have to give a speech in front of all the bigwigs at the end of the evening. I can just imagine being called to say a few words on behalf of the club and telling a blue joke half-pissed. No, a captain's life is not for me.

Daniel went back Down Under in 2008 and Mick

Potter – yet another Australian – came in at the start of the 2009 season. Mick had done great things with Catalan Dragons, taking them to the Challenge Cup Final and being voted Super League's Coach of the Year. It's early days for Mick at the club. And of course, I'm off to pastures new next season. But I wish him all the best – apart from when his team is playing against me!

I'd love to go into coaching when my playing days are over and I'd like to think I can take something from all the coaches I've worked with at Saints: Shaun's tactical awareness, Ellery's team-building skills, Basil's attacking flair and Daniel's defensive know-how. If I can take a little bit of each of them I could be half decent.

Aside from the coaches, no chapter on the men I've worked with would be complete without mention of my best playing pals.

First up, there's Kez Cunningham. They're planning to erect a bronze statue of the great man, probably outside the new stadium, and that says it all, really. When it's up there in all its glory, I'm going to sneak round and tie a bed sheet round him like a big nappy, just for a bit of fun. Kez used to be my drinking buddy, but it got a bit messy for him and he packed it all in. But he's still funnier than ever, a right wit who's always taking the piss. When we go away for games, he's my room buddy and we're like an old married couple with our routines. I always have the bed furthest away from the door and we get up at 8.30am and have our breakfast. He always pours my coffee for me (he's definitely the husband in our relationship). As the wife, I'm usually telling him he can't have a second fry-up or he'll get fat. It's led to the odd sulk, but we never fall out for long!

Kez is the most chilled, laid-back man you could wish to meet socially, but when he gets on the pitch he turns into a caveman on speed. He's hard as nails, but not in a dirty way. I don't think he's been sent off in his entire career. He's a champion bloke whose record speaks for itself. He makes every pundit's dream team, yet he's never won the Man of Steel. What a joke. You play all your career and only have a handful of genuine mates who you'll ring every week for a chat. He's one of them.

Another close pal of mine is good old Martin Gleeson. He joined Saints in 2002 and, even though he was a Wigan lad, I didn't really know him apart from the odd hello when I saw him in town. I remember playing against him when he was at Huddersfield in 2000 and thinking: 'Who's this kid with the great footwork?' The next thing I knew, he was my training partner in the gym. We both like our gym work and for years he's been my gym buddy – and drinking buddy and gambling buddy! Glees is one of the daftest, funniest blokes you could ever meet – and he's like that without trying. He acts all sensible and straight-laced but he's just naturally hilarious.

He's had some nicknames over the years. He was called Tranny for a while because when we grew our hair and he was clean-shaven, he looked like a woman. A hard bastard of a woman, and one you wouldn't dare chat up, but a woman all the same. Basil used to call him The Germ, not because he's unhygienic, it's just that he looks like he needs a wash all the time! But no-one could question his ability on the field. He can step men like they're not there. He can read a game like a half-back and put shots on people like a forward. He was the best player on tour in 2008 when everyone else seemed like they weren't trying. Recently, Glees and I have settled down (shit, not like that – we haven't settled down *together*) and cut down on the mad nights out. Him and his missus Sam are often round our house for nights in and vice versa. Nowadays we're happy with a glass of wine or two and a meal. Salt of the earth, is Glees.

Another pal is Chris Joynt. When I arrived at Saints I used to get a lift to training with Joynty, who's also a Wigan lad. Every journey was a 45-minute lesson on the ways of life – better than any of the lessons I had at school. I loved those days and I used to ask him all sorts of questions about houses, money, and investments – stuff I knew nothing about. Joynty's five years older than me and I suppose he was my rugby uncle in those days.

When I was 21 and without a care in the world, Joynty said I should buy a house and get on the property ladder. I turned to him in the car and said: 'You're joking, aren't you? I love it at my mum's. Dinner on the table, my kit washed every night, my dancing gear ironed.' But he convinced me, saying it was a good time to buy. I took his advice and it was the best thing I could have done at the time. It gave me independence and it worked out great for me financially.

Playing-wise, Joynty was always the calming influence in the dressing room. When people were ranting and raving, he would say in a chilled voice what needed to be done on the field. He said nothing got fixed by being angry. He was a leader by example.

If there's one player who perhaps had it all it was

Jason Robinson. It was amazing the things he could do with the ball in his hands. By nature he was a scrum-half but he was so fucking fast that he found himself out on the wing and then at full-back when he converted to union. I never had any doubt that he'd be a success when he switched codes. Some players make the transition and think it'll be easy, that the games are basically the same. They're similar in many ways but very different in others. But Jason was always looking to learn, get his head down and add even more to his already-awesome game. He always had the brilliance to change a match. He was simply a winner, such a clever player with a scrum-half's brain in a back three player. One of the finest I've played with and against.

Andy 'Faz' Farrell was another one of those very rare players who could do it all. Faz was really a half-back in a big man's body. His distribution was exceptional, he'd fire off flat 20 yard passes right on the money time after time. But, unlike some of us soft half-backs, he was as hard as nails. Probably the ultimate all-round player who could have played anywhere from one to 13 and done a top-class job.

When I was at Wigan, Faz would hang around with a clique of older players even though he's only 18 months older than me. Basically, if you weren't in his posse then he didn't talk to you or laugh at your jokes. Then when you got older and became accepted into the senior clique, it all changed. When I started playing for Great Britain he seemed to warm to me... he even pretended to find my gags funny.

Of all the Saints I've played with, I'd pick out my long-time half-back partner Tommy Martyn as the real gem. Like Jason Robinson, he could work magic to change games. We made a really good partnership at six and seven. He was so skilful and he had a massive rugby brain. He did things that took your breath away and together with a great kicking game he was a perfect ally on the pitch. Although he never appeared to have much pace, when he made the breaks he was rarely caught.

The best import we had at Knowsley Road was Australian Jamie Lyon, who spent a couple of years with us. He took rugby league to another level in my eyes. He'd do things like catch the high ball above his head rather than in the bread basket, something we now take for granted, but he was the first to do it. He didn't look much like a rugby player. He had a bit of a chubby face but the pace he had was incredible and, allied with his skill set, there were some games which he essentially won on his own. I remember a game against Salford when he scored two sensational 60-yard tries, the kind that most players might score once in a career. And then, of course, he was one of the best place-kickers on the planet. A true great.

But if there was one player I envy and who I'd like to be compared with, it's another Aussie, Darren Lockyer. He's awesome with a supreme vision and a stunning kicking game. Shit, he's even good defensively. It's almost like he's playing the game in slow motion; he has so much time. He's played for Brisbane Broncos for almost 15 years and he might not be as fast as he once was, but he's still probably the best rugby league player in the world.

CHAPTER 14

INTERNATIONAL PLAYBOYS

I won my first GB cap in 1997 during a home series, coming off the bench in the third test against the Australians. We lost 37-20, so it was hardly a happy debut. But two years later, at the end 1999 season, I was chuffed to bits to be picked to play in the Tri-Nations tournament in Australia and New Zealand.

But we came last, which was nothing fucking unusual. It was a typically dreadful tour. Everyone made excuses for us but sometimes you've got to take it on the chin and say you're not up to it.

After the last game in New Zealand, me, Adrian 'Moz' Morley and Andy Hay flew back to Sydney and all the rest of the team flew home. The season was over and we were three young lads with no commitments, so we decided to stay on for a holiday.

My mate Owen was backpacking at the time and we met him at the Coogee Bay Hotel. On the first night, we went round Sydney and had a great time chilling out after a hard year of rugby. Sydney is a fab place, full of young people from around the world, all out to have a good time. I've been to the city a few times and I've never seen any trouble.

We ended up at a bar called Bourbon Beef, a 24-hour joint (no pun intended) in the heart of the city's red light area. The streets round there are amazing – full of cool bars, restaurants, nightclubs, strip clubs and sex shops. In the early hours, me and Owen chipped back to the hotel, a little bit worse for wear. We needed to get our heads down because we were due to head up to Newcastle in a few hours to hook up with a few of Moz's old Leeds Rhinos mates.

The journey was about the same as Manchester to London but we had no idea how we were getting there. The next morning, Moz announced he'd met some random Aussie bloke in a bar who said he'd give us all a lift. We went for some lunch in our hotel and Moz rang the guy, who he called 'Fast Eddie', but there was no answer. But Moz is nowt if not persistent and he kept ringing until he finally woke the bloke up.

'Hi Eddie, it's Adrian from last night. You said you would give us a lift to Newcastle.' There was no suggestion of doubt in his voice. It was like he was phoning a taxi. Remarkably, the bloke said he'd pick us up in half an hour – I'd expected him to make some excuse and put the phone down. After all, when you're drunk at four in the morning you say things to strangers that you don't mean. I know I do. But Moz has a way of getting people to do stuff for him.

We quickly packed our bags and sat in the sun outside the hotel, waiting for Fast Eddie. He arrived on time in a dirty white four-litre Holden – it was a big ugly thing that perfectly matched its driver. Fast Eddie was a monster of a man, a huge sweaty creature and I thought: 'What the fuck have we got ourselves involved with here?'

But he was nice and friendly: 'G'day fellas, going to Newcastle eh? I'll look after you.' As I climbed into the back of his filthy motor, I was thinking: 'I'd rather be looked after by Harold Shipman.' Fast Eddie (it wasn't his real name but Moz thought he looked like the guy from *True Romance* and he happily answered to it) stopped off at a petrol station on the highway where they sold beer. We bought two crates for the journey – we were on holiday, after all – and got back on the road. It was gloriously sunny and we sat drinking beer, enjoying the Aussie scenery. Everything was sweet.

We'd only been going a few minutes when Moz asked: 'So, Eddie, what did you get up to last night after I left you?' If I wasn't overly worried about our driver before, I soon would be.

'Well, mate, it's funny you should ask.' The windows were down and Eddie was shouting so that me and Owen could hear in the back. 'I went to this strip joint and I ended up having sex with some chick who had a little cock and balls.' He looked at me and Owen in his rear view mirror and gave us a knowing wink. I glanced over at Owen as if to say: 'Oh God, this man is going to kill us, he's a fucking psycho!' Eddie continued: 'It was a bit of a shock when I saw she wasn't a proper Sheila but you know what it's like, eh fellas?' No, I fucking didn't! He then went into detail about how he did the chick-boy up the wrong 'un.

I drained my beer and quickly cracked open another. I'd seen horror films where travellers had been picked up by weirdos and driven to some remote farm and killed. He probably had his family of in-breds waiting to bum us all before chopping us up into little pieces. If that was going to happen, I wanted to be drunk.

The rest of the journey was fairly quiet, with me, Moz, Andy and Owen drinking cans and looking out of the windows to avoid catching the eye of our strange new friend. I was surprised and relieved when we arrived in Newcastle, having half-expected to be driven to my death. Eddie even rang his pal who ran a B&B, where we could stay the night for cheap while we got our bearings. He dropped us off at his mate's place and that was it, he said bye and drove back to Sydney. I felt a bit bad that I'd judged him purely on the way he looked and his unsavoury sexual habits. He was actually a nice guy who went out of his way for us. Or maybe he saw that four strapping lads would be a bit of a handful back on his murder farm.

The B&B Eddie's friend ran was called The Star Inn and it was without doubt the most Godforsaken place I have ever stayed in. We were all in one room, which we also shared with lots of cockroaches, fleas and mosquitoes. There was a double bed and two singles, and a toilet in the corner. It was how I imagined a Turkish prison cell to be. But it was cheap and it was a roof over our heads for the night.

When we woke up the next day – none of us had malaria which was a nice surprise – we decided to hire a car and drive up to the Gold Coast for a bit of a road trip. Luckily, the Sydney Roosters were interested in signing Moz at the time and so he rang them up and blagged a car. He called up the office and said the Chief Executive had promised him a motor so he could drive round the area and decide whether he wanted to move there. They didn't question it and sent a car, a big Ford saloon, round that afternoon. We headed off up the coast for three weeks. All the Aussie girls loved our accents and we all did well on that front. We spent most of our time round the coast near Brisbane and had the time of our lives.

It was an absolute blast, and we were out partying all the time. After one particularly boozy night, we stumbled out of a nightclub called Shooters at about five in the morning. We headed towards the beach, the four of us having a ball. Me and Moz decided to run off into the sea and do a bit of skinny-dipping. We were starkers and messing about in the sea as the sun came up. But as we came back onto the shore I could see Owen looking a bit edgy. When we got closer – carrying our clothes until we'd dried out – I saw two people stood next to him. They were coppers! One of them said: 'You're in a public place, put your clothes on.' So, I put my T-shirt on and stood there smiling. I was still absolutely smashed from the night before and the policemen were riled. 'Put your pants on too, you idiot.' We did as they asked and we both almost fell over as we tried to get our legs into our trousers. 'You'd better come with us,' the cops said, and we were loaded into the meat van. They drove us to the cop shop, bollocked us and charged us with indecent exposure. It was totally over the top. It was dawn, only just getting light and there was no one about to expose ourselves to. I reckon they were just bored and fancied giving us Poms some grief.

They locked us up for an hour and let us go at about 7am. One of the coppers asked us where we were going and we said: 'Back to our apartment to sleep.' He said: 'Don't do that – you're in court at 9.30am.' He pointed across the road to the Magistrates Court where we had to go.

I said to Moz: 'What do we do? Should we go and get a coffee and wait?' He shook his head and replied: 'I'm fucked if I'm hanging around here for two hours. Let's fuck off to bed.' So we jumped in a cab to the apartment and put our heads down; we didn't show up in court. The following morning, we headed back down to New South Wales to catch our flight home.

We'd only been driving for an hour or so when we were pulled over by the police for speeding. We were doing 120kph, way past the limit, but when Moz showed his licence, the officer said we couldn't get done as Brits over there. He just told us not to do it again and waved us on. Of course, his advice just made us feel free to speed all we wanted and we zoomed past about 50 speed cameras, seeing how many we could make flash. We thought: 'Fuck it, we can't get done.'

We managed to catch our flight home without incident but when we went through customs, me and Moz were bricking it in case there was a warrant out for our arrest over the indecent exposure charge. We later found out that if we'd flown out from Brisbane we'd have probably been pulled, but because we went from a different state we were okay.

A few weeks after we arrived back in England, Moz

got a call from the Sydney City Roosters, saying they'd received dozens of speeding tickets from the car hire company! But he managed to talk his way out of it and he ended up signing for them the following year.

That trip Down Under was typically rubbish for rugby. For me, the international game has almost invariably been about missed opportunities, bad planning, wrong tactics and, ultimately, crushing disappointment. But, as with any trip away from home with a load of like-minded lads, it was great for partying.

Of the many funny tales I remember of international tournaments, the World Cup Challenge in 1997 is one all the lads still talk about. Funnily enough, I made my debut for Saints in that tournament, against Aussie team Cronulla Sharks. It was obviously a massive game for me and one I'll never forget but I won't bore you with all the details. Instead, I'll tell you a funny story that happened on the way to Australia to play our ties Down Under.

We stopped off in Hong Kong and coach Shaun McRae allowed us 48 hours to chill out and relax. We were in the middle of a tough Super League season – our number one priority – and he wanted us to have a break, to enjoy ourselves. And boy, we were up for that.

While in Hong Kong, we were the guests of a millionaire British businessman who ran a bank over there. He was a massive St Helens fan and there was no expense spared. We had a lavish 10-course meal at his bank, with all the free champagne and £200-a-bottle wine we could sup. And believe me, we did some supping. They reckon that after the first bottle of fine wine, you don't appreciate the taste and it's a waste. Well, I wasted a lot of wine. Probably about a grand's worth!

At about 5 o'clock, the rich guy took us down to the harbour where a boat was waiting for us. Again, no expense was spared and there was unlimited free booze and posh food. When we got back on dry land, he said we had two choices: we could either go shopping with his assistants or go with him for a massage. Being a young lad, I thought to myself: 'I've heard of Hong Kong massages, so I'm buggered if I'm going shopping.' A handful of the lads went shopping (why, I don't know) and the rest of us followed the millionaire for a 'massage'.

When we got taken to the massage place – which was as posh as a five-star hotel – we were all a bit pissed and laughing and joking. We were told to have a shower before going for a jacuzzi together. Then it was time to go to our separate rooms for our massages. It was weird, because the rooms weren't really rooms. It was a big hall with high ornamental ceilings, divided by paper partitions. Each 'room' had a bed with a Chinese girl stood next to it, wearing a white nurse-style uniform. I – like my team-mates and various members of the training squad – was stark naked save for a small white towel round my waist. She gave me a massage for about 10 minutes and then turned me over to do my front. I thought: 'I hope I'm right in thinking something fruity is coming here…'

My hopes were realised when, after a few minutes massaging my arms, chest and legs, she whipped off my towel and got down to business. Needless to say, the old boy was already stood to attention and she started doing what she did best. I'd never been in that situation before (and I haven't since) and I was laid there thinking: 'A few months ago I was eating cheese spread butties in the ramshackle Widnes clubhouse and now I'm playing for the Saints and being whacked off in a five-star Hong Kong massage parlour. Get in there!'

Then, while my girl was mid-stroke, I heard an almighty roar of outrage coming from behind the next partition. 'What do you think you're doing? Leave that alone!' It was Apollo Perelini, a giant Samoan and born-again Christian. Looking back, we should have warned him what was likely to happen when we went for our Hong Kong 'massage'. But I guess we were all a bit too pissed to realise.

The paper partitions prevented me from seeing exactly what happened, but I saw enough. Apollo was nicknamed 'The Terminator' because of his hard tackling, and when I saw his shadow through the paper partition, I thought he was going to terminate the poor girl who'd dared touch his pecker. He jumped up, going 'No, no, no!' and sprinted back into the shower area. I don't know whether this is true, but I later heard he ran through two paper walls, leaving behind an Incredible Hulk-style shape in each.

I was laughing my balls off and everyone was shouting to each other: 'What went on there? What's going on?' I yelled back: 'It's okay, Apollo's gone for an early shower.' And then we all went back to business. The Apollo thing got everyone talking as the massage girls were seeing to us. 'What's yours like, Longy?' said one of the lads (I've agreed not to name any of the other people there that afternoon). I didn't reply and just concentrated on the job in hand, as it were.

In my international career – where I had lots of fun off the pitch, but precious little on it – I played five times for England and 15 times for Great Britain. But my only real ambition in all that time was to beat the Australians in their own back yard. I did that in 2006 during the Tri-Nations, a tournament that marked the end of my career at that level. It also got my name in the headlines for all the wrong reasons. I've devoted the next chapter to that sorry – and sometimes amusing – episode.

CHAPTER 15

MESSED UP DOWN UNDER

We were midway through the 2006 Tri-Nations tour and I was 15,000 feet in the air, flying over the Tasman Sea from New Zealand to Australia with my Great Britain team-mates. Oh, and by the way, I was drinking Baileys from a protein shake bottle. A word of advice to any newcomer to international rugby: if you want to continue your airport drinking on a plane without your coach knowing, nothing looks more like a protein shake than Baileys!

We'd just been hammered 34-4 by the Kiwis and it was the beginning of the end of a very up-and-down tour for me. The following day, I flew home on my own with a key game against the Aussies left to play. I landed back at Manchester to be greeted by the press pack and all sorts of allegations. As I shuffled into the arrivals in my flip-flops, unshaven and with bags under my eyes, a journalist asked why I'd returned early. I simply mumbled: 'I just want to go home.' I regretted it the minute I said it, conscious that I sounded like a right soft arse. After that, in all the media excitement that followed, I toed the official line and kept my mouth shut about it all. Until now, that is. Here's what happened...

The Saints and Hull players joined the tour a week after the rest of the GB squad because we'd played in the Grand Final back home. Without us, they played a warm-up friendly against Newcastle (which they won) on Australia's Gold Coast. On the plane over, I was buzzing after my best season for Saints in 10 years, in which I became the only player ever to win a third Lance Todd trophy. During the flight, all I could think about was beating Australia on their home turf. I was at the pinnacle of my domestic career but I had never managed to prove myself at international level. I was determined to do so now. The Super League was over for the season so I could put my rivalry with Wigan on the back burner and focus all that negative energy on the cocky Aussies, who I was desperate to see brought down a peg or two.

I went out on the tour party knowing my performances for Great Britain had always been hit-and-miss. For Saints I'd been all over the show, running the game with a free rein. But different GB coaches had locked me into a slot, usually down the left channel. We'd get to the middle of the field and I'd always been on the left, the stand-off on the right and the 1 and 13 in the middle. That wasn't my game and so this time round I went to the coach, Brian 'Nobby' Noble, and told him that if they wanted to make best use of me I had to play like I played for Saints, with the freedom to run the game. In fairness, Nobby agreed.

After the Newcastle friendly, the gaffers announced that we were all going dragon boat racing as a team-building exercise. Now, dragon boat racing – a big thing Down Under involving paddling like fuck in long canoes with a carved dragon's head at one end – seemed like fun. But we weren't on a bloody stag do. I went to see Nobby and explained that us lads who'd played in the Grand Final had not touched a ball in eight days and needed some ball-in-hand practise. What's more, I wanted the whole team to get on the park and get to know one another from a playing point of view. We had to start working together on some plays. Thankfully, Nobby listened to me and we canned the dragon boat racing in favour of a proper training session.

We got to the session at our base at Manley in Sydney, where, contrary to what I'd hoped, the training was a joke. They had us doing shuttle runs, sit-ups, press-ups, even fucking wrestling. It was all fitness stuff and I was sweating buckets thinking: 'Bugger me, we've all just played a punishing Super League season and we're as fit as butchers' dogs. We don't need fitness training.' We didn't touch a single bloody ball. When we weren't being beasted like Army recruits, we were practising tackle technique. Well, if a team of Great Britain's finest players didn't know how to tackle we really were up shit creek without a paddle (be it a on a dragon boat or otherwise). We wanted to get our hands on the ball and felt tricked, conned by the coach. I remember looking over at Jamie Peacock, the captain, and he was mortified. 'We've been ambushed,' he said. 'They've fucking ambushed us.' Those are not the words you expect your captain to say of the coaching staff. But I totally agreed with him.

Our first of four Tri-Nations games was in Christchurch, New Zealand, the following weekend. But in the days leading up to it, the training got no better; running up and down doing pointless stuff like tackle tech. We didn't need all that crap. We all played for different Super League teams and we needed to learn to play as a unit. But despite having a whole week to do this, we didn't properly discuss role-play and game tactics until the morning before the bloody game!

They got us all up at 10am, despite the fact that we weren't playing till the evening. Normally, when you have a late kick-off, you can have a long lie-in. All players are different, but some (me included) like to stay in bed in order to be fresh for the game. But they didn't let us make that decision and everyone had to be up and at it by 10. They took us to a field that was basically just a dirty patch of grass where you'd expect cows to graze.

I have bad ankles and as I surveyed our training field – where most Sunday league footballers would fear to tread – I thought: 'Jesus fucking Christ!' So, we stood there and listened as the coaching team told us our strategy a few hours before we were about to face the Kiwis. I said to the lads next to me: 'We should have been talking match tactics four days ago.' It's crucial that the players have time to talk about the plan, add our feedback and change the odd thing to match the strengths and abilities of the squad. It's all about getting things right with talk and practise. Leaving it to the day of the game was like taking your driving test on the morning of your 17th birthday after watching a few hours of *Top Gear*.

Anyway, they announced the strategies after getting

us all up like Scouts at camp. The conditions were embarrassing and we were all stood there, listening to the coaching staff tell us how they wanted us to play later that day. I thought to myself: 'What are we doing? Have I been dreaming the last ten years of my life and I'm actually a Sunday pub league footballer?' I caught Wello's eye and he went: 'Those words are just like blah, blah, blah.' Looking back, I think even then I wanted to bugger off home.

We played New Zealand on 10 October and lost, though considering the preparation, we performed quite well. They beat us 18-14 but I think if we'd had some proper prep, we'd have won that game.

The mood in the camp was really down. We had all been given special Tri Nations diaries so we could write down our thoughts. One of the entries in mine reads: 'This is a total fuck-up. I want to say something but I'll wait until after the Aussie game. It's no good battling with the bosses and upsetting the camp.' I was getting more and more frustrated but I remained tight-lipped.

In the build-up to the Australia game on 4 November, things picked up a bit and we were starting to gel as a team. But I was still on a downer. I was in a shopping mall one afternoon with my Saints mates Gilly and Leon Pryce. We were walking along and I saw a pregnant woman with a kid in a pushchair. It made me think of Claire and my young family and I felt really homesick. I don't think I would have missed home so much if things were going better on the tour. If training had been better, my attitude would have been more positive and my mood brighter; I'm sure I wouldn't have missed home as much.

I said to Leon and Gilly: 'I'm thinking about fucking off home.' I told them I was missing my family and that I wasn't enjoying it. Gilly bet me £100 that I wouldn't go home but I told him: 'Keep your money, mate. It hasn't worked out and I'm not enjoying it.' But I slept on it and decided to play the first game against the Aussies before flying home.

The morning we got back to Manley to prepare for our Aussie game, the lads and I went down to Bondi beach. It was a drab, drizzly day and the place was swarming with flies. There was graffiti everywhere and the shops looked shabby when the sun wasn't shining. We expected it to look like the Aussie beaches you see on telly, but there were no surfers or gorgeous chicks, just us lot. We were all laughing and Leon said: 'Fuck me, Bondi is shit. Blackpool's better than this.' That night, we all had a few beers in the local boozers and we were singing: 'Blackpool's better than Bondi! Blackpool's better than Bondi!' Wello was stood on a table outside out hotel, chanting those very words to passers-by. Thankfully, they were mostly tourists or we might have had a brawl on our hands!

Later that week, Leon did an interview with a British journalist who was covering the tour, and told him what we'd all been singing. He thought it would just be in the UK papers, but the Aussie press got hold of it and they were really pissed off. They kicked off big-style, saying we were taking the piss. They were keen to point out how much better Australia is compared with Britain.

Because Leon's from Bradford, one Aussie paper carried pictures of the 2001 Bradford riots, with cars and shops on fire. Opposite those photos, they had snaps of stunning girls in bikinis posing on Bondi beach. Another rag had similar pictures of gorgeous Australian beach babes alongside photos of a piss-wet view of Blackpool promenade. Leon's comments (which, to be fair, we all agreed with) really wound the Aussie papers up. And it clearly got under the skin of their team because when we played them they seemed more interested in fighting us than playing a game of rugby.

Within seconds of kick-off at the Aussie Stadium in Sydney, I sussed that our opponents weren't their usual cool, collected selves. Instead, they tried to strike off and fight. We started strongly and dominated possession and territory in the first few minutes before man mountain Willie Mason punched Stu Fielden in the face, breaking his nose. Looking back, it was a crazy thing to do but I – a 5ft 9in half-back – squared up to Mason – a 6ft 5in 18-stone prop – and asked him what the fuck he was playing at. Luckily, JP spared me a battering by storming in for a more evenly-weighted brawl with the big fella.

Referee Ashley Klein – an Australian – clearly saw what had happened with Stu but decided to let Mason off with a mild bollocking. Given the green light to do what the fuck he wanted, Mason – no doubt as pissed off as the Aussie newspapers – attacked me 10 minutes into the game. I'd put in a long kick and he came in late with an elbow to the head and a knee to the thigh. I felt like a truck had hit me. My eyebrow was pissing blood and the doc came on and stapled my wound. I wasn't too concerned about the cut and I carried on. It was the nasty dead leg the beast had given me that I was worried about. The ref (did I mention that he was Australian?) let Mason off with another slapped wrist.

I wasn't going to let Mason bully me and it just made me more determined to fuck his team over. But it looked like my international curse still hung over me when, after 28 scoreless minutes, Ben Hornby intercepted a pass from me to set up Greg Inglis for a 70-metre sprint to the line. I thought it was going to be one of those nights but I soon made up for the interception with a break that laid on a try for Wello.

It was 6-6 at half-time and we were soon ahead when JP forced his way over from close range. The Aussies hit back through skipper Darren Lockyer but Gilly put us back in front with a try from nothing. But then I missed a simple penalty and a drop-goal effort and I was thinking it could go the home team's way with a couple of late Houdini-style tries. But three minutes before time I broke from deep to set up a cracking try by Gareth Raynor. Then, in the dying seconds of the game, I was lucky enough to have the chance to stick two huge fingers up at Mason and his angry chums with a drop goal. The whistle went and we were the 12-23 winners. The Aussies thought they could steamroller us in a thug-fest but they couldn't have been more wrong. We held our nerve and played some really good rugby to beat them in their own back yard for the first time in 18 years. If the Aussies had played a fair game, I don't think the feeling of victory would have been half as sweet.

It was easily my best international performance and I was named man of the match. I'll always think of that game as one of the highlights of my career but with hindsight I reckon I'd taken on too much by going on that tour in the first place. I remember waking up the day after the game and feeling like I'd been involved in a car crash. I had whiplash, a dead leg from hell and I could hardly move. Despite the fantastic result I'd always dreamed of, I felt surer than ever that I was going home before my team-mates. I'd just played a long Super League season all the way through to a Grand Final, and now my body and mind were wrecked.

In the week leading up to our second Kiwi test on November 11, I still had a dead leg so I couldn't train properly. My head wasn't with it, either. I really didn't want to be there but the mood in the camp was high after the Aussie win and the general consensus was: 'We can do this.' I decided to stick it out for the sake of the team. I didn't have the heart to announce, 'Right, I'm off' when everyone was really optimistic about our chances. But I should have at least gone to Nobby and told him how I was feeling. I should have asked him to leave me out of the next game against the Kiwis while I got myself together. I can't blame Nobby for not knowing how I was feeling on the inside because I always looked so cheerful on the outside.

We flew out to Wellington to prepare for the next test, but when we got there it was a familiar story. The facilities were crap and we were training on an amateur field. Aussie rugby league commentator Phil Gould wrote a big article in one of the papers over there, calling us 'a bunch of amateurs'. He was a bit harsh. I reckon First Division would have been fairer. I wrote in my diary at the time: 'Phil Gould has been slagging us off, saying we're amateur team. But he has a point – the fat prick.'

Leon and me had been on fire for Saints that year,

with me at scrum half and him partnering me at stand off. In the first New Zealand game, Nobby played Leon on the wing, which was out of position for him, and we lost. For the Australia game he paired us back to six and seven and we demolished them. Yet, despite proving that our deadly Super League partnership worked brilliantly on an international level, Nobby decided it would be a good idea to split us up for the second Kiwi game. He moved Leon back onto the wing to replace an injured Brian Carney. That would have been fair enough if there was no one else to take Brian's place, but Nobby had a substitute winger, Martin Aspinwall, raring to have a go. What's the point in bringing extra wingers on tour if you're not going to use them? I'm not suggesting that I or any player should be picking the team but some things just seem so obvious. It was those kind of issues that made playing international rugby so frustrating. I felt the gaffers didn't give us a fighting chance. If it wasn't bad prep, it was ludicrous team choices.

Predictably enough, New Zealand hammered us 34-4. They ran in six tries to our one at the Westpac Stadium in Wellington. We'd gone in cocky after the Aussie win and our forwards couldn't handle their forward pack. We played shite, defending on the back foot all the time. Afterwards, we were all gutted. I snapped my bicep in that game and my body was an absolute wreck. I decided then that I was going home for definite. I wasn't hanging around for the final match against Australia.

As our coach pulled up at the hotel in Wellington at about 10pm, Nobby grabbed the senior players: me, JP,

Brian Carney, Keith Senior, Moz and said to us: 'Right lads, I don't think you should be having a drink, let's get ourselves right to beat Australia again.' He warned us: 'I know you're all down after the last game and I don't want you drowning your sorrows in alcohol.'

I was knackered so I didn't want to go boozing anyway. To be fair, we'd been out there for three weeks and we'd all stayed off the ale, bar a pint or two with dinner. Some of the lads were going to Wello and Leon's room and I agreed to meet them after visiting the doc for some sleeping tablets. My mind's always hyper after a game and I really needed a good night's rest so I took three to make sure I was right before the flight back to our base in Sydney the following day. The pills were already kicking in when I went up to see the lads. There was about eight of us in Wello's room, all laid out and watching telly and stuff. I decided I'd chill with them until I felt really sleepy and then I'd go down the corridor to my room.

Wello rang room service for some beers and Leon ordered a few bottles of red wine. I was laid there with heavy eyes when Leon asked me if I fancied a drink. 'Yeah, I'll have a glass of wine.' Well, hallelujah, that's the last fucking thing I remember. I'm told we necked the beer and wine, then ordered loads more and supped them, too. Before long (apparently), we'd been partying along the corridor and ended up in Tez Newton's room. I have no recollection whatsoever but I'm told we had a full-on party with blaring music and more booze. We were smashed. So much for the sober night we'd promised Nobby!

I was sharing a room with my Saints pal James 'Robes'

Roby and the next morning he went down for breakfast, leaving me bollock-naked (no surprise there) and star-fished on my bed. He followed a path of discarded clothes along the corridor and, thinking nothing of it, went into the lift where he found one of his T-shirts on the floor. He immediately thought: 'That's got to be Longy.' It was bound to be me but I couldn't remember a thing. Apparently, I was wearing Robes's clothes and throwing them around everywhere. All the stuff in the corridor was his.

I came to when Robes was packing his stuff and cursing me. With a thumping head and a mouth as dry as a nun's chuff, I croaked: 'Jesus, Robes, what was I drinking last night?' As he folded his wine-stained clothes into his suitcase, he replied: 'God knows, mate. But you obviously decided you didn't like your own wardrobe.' I didn't have a clue what he was on about and I was too ill to care so I just rolled my aching body over and continued my dream about what I'd do to Willie Mason if left alone with him with a pair of pliers and a blow torch (assuming the big fella was drugged and tied up, of course!)

When I next woke up, Robes had gone and I was running late for the coach to the airport. In a zombie-like state (sleeping tablets and booze really don't mix) I somehow managed to get showered, pack my stuff and stumble down to the hotel reception.

My first clear memory is being in the departure lounge at Wellington airport. Me and Glees were sat at a table with Wilko and his parents who'd come for a holiday and to watch us play. They had a bottle of red wine and I had a glass as a livener. It's true what they say about the hair of the dog and by the time I'd finished my second glass I was feeling brand new again.

The wine had done its work but before I had a chance to go to the bar to buy the Wilko family a drink back, they announced our plane was boarding and everyone made their way to the gate. I had a few New Zealand dollars left on me so me and Glees went to Duty Free and bought a bottle of Baileys. We emptied it into a protein shake bottle and ran to join our pals. In the queue for the plane, me, Glees and Leon passed the bottle round, getting dafter with every sip. We hadn't drunk that much at the airport but it didn't take much to top up what we'd supped the night before.

We found our seats on the plane and I was chuffed to be right behind my good pal Wello, who was suffering from a severe hangover. After several flicks to his ears, the plane started taxiing towards the runway and Wello put his head in his hands and said: 'Fucking hell, this is going to be a long flight.' It was probably the longest four hours of his life.

Once we were in the air, we calmed down and nodded off. But about 20 minutes later, Leon woke up to find he was the only one awake and he decided to stick his iPod headphones on me and crank up the volume. I woke up with a start, cracked him in the ribs, and took a long swig of Gleeson's 'protein shake'. I was back on it, big-style!

Obviously, if me and Leon were awake, Glees had to be too and before we knew it, we were all singing, being daft and torturing Wello by slapping him on the back of the head. We weren't overly loud but everything is magnified on a plane and we were getting a few funny looks, so we calmed down before anyone complained and went back to sleep. The next thing I knew we'd touched down and Glees was hitting me across the face with one of my flip-flops.

We got off the plane and went through passport control. Me, Glees and Leon got a bit of shit off the rest of the lads for spoiling their sleep and there were a few pissed-off head shakes from other passengers, but apart from that, all seemed okay.

However, when our coach pulled up at the hotel at about 10pm, Nobby took me to one side and said: 'Look, I wasn't very happy about your behaviour on the plane. There have been some complaints from the other passengers.' It turned out there were a load of Germans on our flight who didn't appreciate our boisterous behaviour.

Nobby reminded me of his warning not to go drinking after the New Zealand game. I nodded back and thought: 'I don't remember a bloody thing.' I recalled having a glass of wine after my sleepers but the rest – including the flight – was a blur. I apologised for being daft on the plane but stressed that you do stupid things when you mix sleepers with booze. Then I added: 'To be honest with you Nobby, I'm fucking off home. It's not just popped into my head now because I'm in bother, I've been thinking about it for a while.' He was surprised at what I said, I think he was just expecting me to apologise for my behaviour on the plane. 'Don't be like that, Sean,' he said. But I replied: 'It's nothing to do with you, mate, I just want to go home, I'm not enjoying it. My head's been in bits for ages. I knew yesterday that I wouldn't be hanging around for the Australia game, that's why I had a drink.'

He wasn't expecting me to be on such a downer and he told me not to go home. I said: 'I tell you what, I'm going to go out tonight and I'm going to have a beer or two.' He said: 'Yeah go on, go out tonight, get it out of your system and we'll talk about it tomorrow.' I said: 'Okay Nobby, I'll have a drink tonight but I'm still going home tomorrow.' He was having none of it and replied: 'We'll carry on this conversation in the morning when you're not being silly.'

I walked into the hotel restaurant where the bloke who fixed the flights – his name was Jimmy – was sat eating. I said: 'Jimmy, get me on a plane tomorrow, I'm fucking off home.' Next, I rallied up the troops – Glees and a few of the Saints lads – and explained to them that I was leaving early. My mates weren't surprised; I'd hinted plenty of times that I wanted to go. I left them at the bar and went upstairs to my room and rang Daniel Anderson, my gaffer back at Saints. 'Daniel, I'm coming home,' I told him. He sighed, no doubt wondering what the fuck I'd been up to, then replied: 'Oh no, you haven't done anything bad have you?' I could detect the worry in his voice. I reassured him: 'No, I've been thinking about it for a while. I'm just fed up.' He said: 'Well, if you've made your mind up, get yourself home. Just be aware that it will come out in the papers.' I asked him if he minded, and he said no. Next, I rang my missus and then went back down to the bar to have a farewell booze with the lads.

There were about a dozen of us – half the squad – and we went down to a pub near the hotel and had a load of pints and a laugh. Everyone got leathered and the mood was upbeat. They all knew I was going but we didn't really talk about it; everyone was looking forward to stuffing the Australians again and I was the least of their concerns.

At about 1am, we staggered back to the hotel. I was taking the piss out of the others because they all had a training session first thing in the morning but, even then, most of them doubted that I'd actually go. After all, even before the glorious Aussie game I'd been telling my closest friends – Glees, Leon and Gilly – that I was going to bugger off but I hadn't. I realised how drunk I was when I got to my room and could barely get the key card through the slot. But I eventually got the door open and collapsed on my bed. When I woke up the following morning I noticed Wilko – my roommate – had already left for training. I also noticed that I'd pissed the bed! But, let's face it, that was hardly a one-off and I went about my usual routine of sorting it out. I took the pee-soaked sheets off the bed and hung them out to dry on the balcony. Then I had a shower and packed my bags. Once those jobs were done, I lay down on Wilko's piss-free bed and had a nap before leaving for my flight.

I'd only been asleep a few minutes when there was a loud knock on the door. It was JP – the captain – and his vice-captain Brian Carney. I let them in and JP said: 'What's going on, Longy?' I replied: 'You must have heard, I'm going home.' He said: 'Yeah, the Saints were saying at training that you were fucking off, but surely that's not right. We need you for the Australia game. Come on lad, hang on for a week and help us beat the Aussies. Then we'll be in the final.' JP would run his blood to water for his country. He is a smashing lad and a great captain so I listened to what he had to say. But my mind was made up. 'You can say what you want but I'm going. I haven't made it up on the spur of the moment, I've been thinking about it for three weeks. I'm out of here.' JP just sighed. He was one of the boys and if there was one person who could have changed my mind, it was him. But it was never going to happen and they left me to it and went downstairs.

Minutes later, there was another knock on the door. It was Nobby. JP had been downstairs and told him he'd failed to persuade me to stay. 'Can we have a chat, Sean?' he said when he walked into the room. I lay back down on Wilko's bed and prepared myself for a lecture. Then – and I will never forget that moment as long as I live – he laid down on my piss-soaked mattress! He said: 'I think you are being a bit rash, son. I know you're having negative thoughts but you've got to stick it out. I have given you free rein to run the team how you want and we can beat Australia again. I want you to give it another go.'

Before I had a chance to respond, he reached down and felt his shorts. 'What's up with this bed?' he asked. I replied: 'Yeah, sorry about that, Nobby. I pissed it last night.' As though ignoring what I'd just told him, he casually moved off the mattress while remaining as cool as possible. He didn't change his position and literally slid off the bed and onto the floor. When he landed on the deck, he was still on his side, his elbow on the carpet and his head rested on his hand – he reminded me of David Brent from *The Office* when he's trying to look cool before having his photo taken. Not a word was said about the fact his bare legs had been lying in my piss. I was thinking: 'Brilliant, this is fucking brilliant.' Nobby, seemingly unmoved by the fact that one side of his shorts was wet with urine, said: 'I've given you the chance to run the team and play the way you want to play, so you need to stick it out.' At that point Wilko came through the door. Because of the layout of the room, all he could see was my empty bed and Nobby lying on his side on the floor. But before he walked any further, Nobby held his hand out and said: 'Give us five, Jon.'

Wilko made himself scarce and Nobby and me had a good heart-to-heart. I told him how I felt about everything and that I wasn't going to change my mind.

As Nobby left the room, he said: 'I think you're making a mistake, Sean. There's a fine line between a genius and a madman.' He then got up and left, leaving me thinking: 'Has he just called me a genius or a nutter?'

The minute Nobby had gone, I rang Wilko on his mobile. 'Do me a favour,' I said. 'Order me a taxi on the quiet and get them to pick me up round the back of the hotel.' He sorted it and I managed to leave the building without a fuss. When I got to the airport, I had just minutes to spare so I had to run to the gate to catch my plane. I hadn't spoken to my wife since the previous night and she had no idea what flight I was on. But she probably assumed Nobby and the lads would persuade me to stay.

I was knackered on the flight home and slept most of the way. During the few hours that I was awake, I thought about seeing my family and wondered how the lads would do in the final game against the Aussies (they ended up losing). I didn't really see it as a big deal that I was flying home early. I felt tired but relaxed when I stood by the luggage carousel at Manchester Airport. But then a bloke in a fluorescent vest came up to me and asked: 'Are you Sean Long?' I nodded and he said: 'I've been asked to warn you that there are a lot of reporters and photographers waiting for you out there.' I said what I usually say in such circumstances: 'Fuck.' I asked if they could sneak me out another way, but he laughed and said: 'We only do that for people like the Prime Minister.'

Luckily, once I'd gone past the newspaper and TV people, there was a guy from the RFL waiting for me and he drove me home. When I got in, I kissed Claire and Olivia and then switched on *Sky Sports News* to see what was being said about me. After a few minutes, there was footage of me, pushing my luggage trolley and telling reporters: 'I just want to go home.' I cringed as I watched it and said to Claire: 'You're married to a dick.'

I went to bed that night knowing my international rugby career was over. I had never put it high in my priorities because at international level, the game was shit. Don't get me wrong, I always gave 100 per cent when I pulled on the GB or England jersey but the international game was a shambles. There was never enough preparation and I felt that successive coaches never worked to individual players' strengths. People, usually those who've never played the sport or the attention-seeking retired ones looking to stir up controversy, say you should be playing for your country just for the love of it. What bollocks.

I came home from the 2006 tour 'in disgrace', and feeling physically and mentally shattered. How much did I get paid for my trouble? My return for that trip was about 1600 quid. Look at my good mate Kez Cunningham. He dislocated his elbow playing for GB against New Zealand in 2002 and it nearly ended his career. Do they come chasing after you asking what they can do to help? Do they fuck. People forget that this is my job and that if I can't play rugby league then I can't provide for my wife and kids.

I've never had any regrets about quitting international rugby. I definitely think it's helped prolong my career. Top-level rugby puts an incredible strain on body and mind. You need to have a complete close season off to recover. That final tour proved it. I was still knackered when the 2007 season started because I hadn't had the necessary rest and I had a shit year. It's not rocket science, we're not machines. You've read elsewhere in this book about the injuries I've suffered through my career. That amount of physical damage and repair takes its toll.

CHAPTER 16
SEAN OF THE DEAD

I'm currently recovering from the worst of the three broken jaws I've had in my career.

It happened on 3 July – a month ago as I write this – when we were playing Salford away (it was a shit game that we lost 20-10). Early in the second half, we had them penned in their own corner and I raced off the line. As I went in to tackle their winger, he put his head up and accidentally nutted me square on the chin. I knew immediately something was up. The skin had split and blood was pissing out, but I wasn't too bothered about that; a bit of blood was the least of my problems. When I closed my mouth, my teeth didn't meet. The bottom row had moved more than an inch to the left while the top half were where they're meant to be. I put my hands to my face and tried to push my lower jaw back in line, but the pain was unbearable. Despite knowing more than the average bloke about broken jaws, I'm no surgeon. I gestured towards the physio and he came straight over. He said: 'What's the matter?' Speaking like a ventriloquist, I replied: 'I've broken my jaw.' He had a quick look at my face and said: 'Bloody hell, let's get you off.'

I knew straight away that it was more serious than my other jaw breaks. With the others, the teeth stayed in line and I had simply cracked the bone. This time it was a proper break, not just some girly hairline fracture. It was bad, really bad, but as I walked off the pitch I wasn't in much pain at all. The adrenaline was keeping it at bay. But when I got to the doctor's room and sat on the medical bench, the pain hit me in a huge rush. It was excruciating. If I so much as tried to talk I was in absolute agony. I was rushed into hospital and they kept me in overnight in case I needed an emergency op. But they didn't operate and I was sent home in the morning.

Because it was such an awkward break, fixing it was a fiddly job. There aren't many surgeons up to it and the first one they asked – a guy in Liverpool – turned it down because he didn't feel confident he could do it. As you might imagine, having a top surgeon bottle out of working on my injury hardly lifted my spirits! Luckily, there was a bloke in Manchester, Stuart Clarke, who felt up to the challenge. He warned me there would be a bit of nerve damage after such a tricky operation, but he was confident he'd do a good job and get my teeth fitting well. From breaking my jaw to having it fixed, I had a week-long wait, just sitting in the house, watching telly and feeling sorry for myself. I couldn't eat for the first three days and when I eventually could, all I managed was the odd messy mouthful of my baby son James's blended food.

Then it was operation time. The surgeon did a really good job but I didn't expect there to be as much nerve damage as there is. As I write this last bit of the book, I have, in the words of my amused Saints mate Gilly: 'A face like a dropped pie'. I can't close my left eye, my left eyebrow won't move and when I speak only one half of my mouth moves. Basically, one side of my face is frozen like I've had a bad stroke. Because I can't close my left eye, it's quite freaky for Claire and the kids, especially when I'm asleep. When you're in deep sleep your eyes roll upwards, so when I'm asleep with one eye open, all you can see is white. It's like something out of a bloody horror film! The nerves are getting slightly better by the day but it's much worse than anyone thought it would be. The docs reckon it should be about right by Christmas. It's August now and I hope they're right. God, don't let it be permanent!

I was allowed home the day after surgery and I was really tender and groggy for a few days. I was also really freaked out by the state of my face. But after about a week, I got used to it and decided that if I was going to play again this year I had to go into work. It had been a fortnight since the accident and that was already too long to be out of training. I had to do some weights to keep up my strength and fitness, scary face or not.

I arrived early for training that Thursday morning and I was in the dressing room chatting to our kit men, Stan Wall and Ian Harris, who were really nice and sensitive with me after seeing the state of my face. But such kindly behaviour was short-lived. A few minutes later, my team-mates Leon and Gilly walked in and they had a fucking field day. 'Jesus! It's SEAN OF THE

DEAD!' quipped my sympathetic old pal Leon. They were in stitches and I mumbled back: 'Yeah, yeah, very funny.'

I'd seen myself in the mirror so I knew why they found me so amusing. As a result, when they laughed, I laughed. And when I laughed, they laughed even harder because my laugh was so funny. One half of my face was laughing, while the other side just stayed frozen, with a wide, unblinking eye staring out. Every player who came into the dressing room that morning took the piss and had a right laugh at me. And to be honest, I'm glad they did. If they'd all felt sorry for me and made a big deal of it, I would have felt much worse. Ruthless piss-taking can be a tonic at times like that. It helps you put things in perspective. I'm stuck with a comedy horror face for a few months but there are many folk out there far, far worse off than me.

Every Monday at Saints, the 'Goose Award' is presented to the player who's done the funniest or most embarrassing thing the week before; be it a fuck-up in training or something stupid while out at the weekend with the lads. Any of us can nominate a winner – or, rather, loser – of the Goose Award and the recipient is decided before we go into training. The nominee that gets the loudest cheer off all the lads wins, and as a 'prize', the poor bastard has to wear a mankini like the one worn by Sacha Baron Cohen in the movie *Borat*. For those of you who haven't seen the film, the outfit in question is basically a skimpy lime green leotard-cum-thong, and it's bloody humiliating for its wearer. Regardless of the weather, the 'winner' has to run around with his meat and two veg almost hanging out, his arse cheeks on full display, generally looking like a prize dickhead. And he has to wear it for a full week! To boot, the outfit is finished off with luminous green sweatbands. It's a God-awful thing to be awarded and, surprisingly enough, I've never won it.

Anyway, on my first Monday back after the jaw op, the lads got to the end of their nominations and the funny tales that went with them. Then Gilly – the tight, big-nosed fucker – stood up and said: 'I nominate Longy for having a face like a dropped pie.' While everyone in the dressing room rolled around laughing, I looked at him and scowled, but in doing so, I backed up his argument. When you scowl, your eyes close a bit. My right eye did, but my left eye remained wide open. Gilly laughed more, as did everyone else, and he said: 'There, I rest my case.' I laughed as well but I was thinking: 'You bastard, Lee Gilmour.'

Gilly's nomination went down so well that I felt sure I'd be awarded the Goose. But I wasn't going to add to my woes by spending a week dressed like a twat. So I had to quickly think up a story that would make one of the other players look like a complete arse and an even worthier winner than me. I said: 'I've got a funny tale about Gary Wheeler.' Gary's one of the young lads in the squad; he plays stand off and he's only 19. I continued: 'Gary came up to me the other day and asked what it's like to be married. He knew I was happily married and wanted a bit of advice about relationships with women. I gave young Gary the benefit of my experience and told him that any long-term relationship with a lady has its peaks and troughs.' As the lads listened, I added: 'And then Gary, bless him, said to me: "Yeah, I know what you mean, Longy, my relationships have all been pigs and troughs."' Everyone erupted into laughter and for the first time since I'd been back, they weren't laughing at me. Gary was mortified and he was protesting: 'That's bollocks – he's made that up. That conversation never happened! I have never said anything about pigs and bloody troughs!' I was equally passionate when I replied: 'Oh, come on Gary, stop telling lies. You came to me in this very dressing room the other day. There's no use denying it now!' As the poor lad sat there, feeling terribly wronged, I thought: 'That was a sly trick to play on the youngster.' But I didn't feel bad for long. After all, you've got to look after number one in this world and sometimes you have to play dirty.

There were four nominations that morning and Gary got the loudest cheer. As he accepted his Goose, he gave me a look and I winked at him with my good eye. He smiled back and accepted his fate like a man. Gary's a sound lad and he showed there that he's a good enough sport to do well in the game, both on and off the field.

I'm back training now, but I'm doing strictly non-contact stuff. I wear an orange bib so everyone knows not to touch me, and I'm concentrating on ball work and fitness. It will be a good while yet before I'm doing tackle tech and the like. The lads have a lot of fun with me in training and their favourite nickname for me is Sloth, after the one-eyed freak from *The Goonies*, who lives underground in the mountain where the kids go hunting for treasure. The tight sods come up to me and say: 'You've been bad, mamma!' in homage to one of the film's catchphrases. It's a good job I'm not the sensitive type.

A couple of months before my jaw injury, I learned that my long stint as a Saints player was coming to an end. In all the time I've been at the club, my contracts have always been for two years at least. And whenever they were due for renewal, the bosses came to me to sort out a new deal. We'd always have it signed and sealed by the end of March, but this year I'd heard nothing. Six weeks later, when other players were comparing their new contracts, I'd still heard nowt and I was wondering what the fuck was going on.

I rang Eamonn, the chairman, and reminded him that my contract was due for renewal. We met the following day and when I sat down in his office, he got straight to the point: 'Look, Sean, we can offer you a one-year deal, not two, and it will be less money. If you accept it, it will probably be the last contract you sign with us.' He said I was free to speak to other clubs to see what other deals were out there. Then he added: 'Come back in three weeks when you've seen who else is interested and we'll all put our cards on the table. We'll sort it out that way.'

The next day, I did an interview with Radio Five Live reporter Stuart Pyke, a guy I know and trust. I said I was open to offers from other clubs and within a week of the interview being broadcast, I had four interested in signing me – Wakefield, Huddersfield, Hull and my old chums Wigan.

The clubs contacted me directly; it didn't take much in the close-knit world of Super League to get hold of my mobile number. Within a week, I had three clubs interested. Wakefield were first to get in touch and I had a meeting with them. The following morning, Huddersfield coach Nathan Brown rang me up. A few days after that, I met with Richard Agar, the Hull boss. I told all three of them what Saints had offered me and left them to decide what they could come up with.

But of the three, it was Richard, the Hull gaffer, who was most on my wavelength. It felt right when I met him. He told me the direction he wanted to take the team and the role he wanted me to play. I was key to Hull's future, he said, and if I signed for them, I would continue to run the show on the field as I'd done for years at Saints. I knew then that unless someone came in with a mega-deal, I'd soon be a Hull FC player. Richard asked if I thought the geography would be a problem, with Hull being so far away from Wigan. I said I'd speak to Claire, but I didn't see it being an issue. He asked me about money and who my agent was, but to be honest, I hadn't really thought that side of things through. I'd been with the same club for 12 years and I know our chairman Eamonn better than any agent, so I always dealt directly with him when it came to my salary. I've never felt comfortable bartering over money; I find that kind of thing embarrassing. But I realised I had to get myself an agent, and fast.

Richard and I agreed to meet again when I'd thought about the salary and I immediately rang Andy Clarke, a mate of mine who is agent to a lot of Super League players. Andy took me on and it all happened really quickly. I had that first meeting with Richard on the Wednesday and by the following Saturday there was an offer on the table.

Then, at the last minute, Wigan came in and said they were keen to sign me. The prospect of going back to my old club, the dastardly rivals I'd loved to hate for so many years, was a strange one. But you know what they say; it's only a game and I was happy to pull on the cherry and white shirt once more if the deal was right. Games against Saints would be quite interesting, though. Being willed on by the Wigan fans while the Saints faithful wished me dead would be a stark change. But as I've said before, I love all that shit so it was never going to faze me. Oh, and the fact that Wigan train about 100 yards from my house wouldn't hurt!

I left it to Andy to get a bidding war going and get me the best deal. And he was brilliant; he really made things happen. Wakefield and Huddersfield couldn't match the other two, so they went on the back burner. A few days later, Andy rang me to say Hull had offered the best package by far (meaning two fingers up to Wigan, which was nice). Hull were even willing to provide me with a house over there so I'd have a home from home and wouldn't be commuting up and down the M62 all the time. It also meant that Claire and me would have a permanent place we could make nice for when she and the kids came to stay. Hull offered me a two-year deal and Andy rang Saints to see if they'd budge on the original offer. Eamonn was honest straight away and said: 'No, we can't. I think you should take the Hull offer.' And we did. It was great that Saints let me shop around while still playing for them. Normally, you can't sign to another club until 1 August. But if the chairman or the owner gives permission and you do it publicly, it's okay. It's very rare a club will allow a player to do that and I owe a lot to my old club for that. I've been a Saint almost all my playing life and they looked after me to the end. I could have been in limbo at the end of the season if they hadn't been so cool with me.

It was hard when Saints decided to release me after a dozen years, but I completely understand their decision. Old buggers like me need to let the new talent in. And financially, the club will save money with youngsters; after all, running a Super League club is like running any other business.

They've got a couple of talented young lads willing and able to wear my number seven shirt – though they might want to wash it first! There's 20-year-old Kyle Eastmond, who's playing for the under 21s. He's played a few very impressive first team games and he's a good lad. He'll probably be there for the next five to ten years if it works out for him. He's hot favourite to take over from me next season. We've also got a young 'un called Matty Smith, who's currently on loan to Celtic Crusaders. He could come back and do the honours. I think they are pushing for Kyle; he's quite an exciting talent and he's currently doing a good job filling my boots while I'm off injured. And, unlike me, he's got his feet on the ground. In fact, Kyle's my complete opposite. At his age I was out of control, but he's teetotal and leads a super-clean life that my old bosses back at Wigan wished I'd done back in those reckless days.

At Hull, Richard wants me to go in there and boss the team. It's an exciting time for me. They've got some good players and, as well as me, they've made five new signings for next year; they are really making a go of it. Hull's a big city and it's a new challenge. I can't wait.

I got a taste of things to come when, just a week after I'd signed for Hull, Saints played them in a Friday night away game at my new club's KC Stadium. As I walked out of the tunnel, I didn't know what the fuck to expect. It was an experience I'd never had before. I ran onto the pitch with both sets of fans cheering me. The Hull fans were singing my name and the Saints crowd were doing the same. Since it was announced that I'm leaving Knowsley Road, the Saints fans have been terrific. I've had pints bought for me and I'm always being stopped in the street by folk wishing me all the best.

I reckon I'll see out my playing days with the Humberside boys and then hopefully move on to coaching. I've been working on my coaching badges for a few years now and I reckon I could be quite good at it. I've told Richard about my aspirations and he's keen for me to work with the young half-backs at the club.

To be honest, if I don't stay on in rugby I don't know what the fuck I'll do with myself. I live and breathe the game and when I'm not training or playing, I'm watching it on the telly or talking about it. The idea of hanging up my rugby boots for good once I stop playing makes me feel a bit lost. Coaching will keep my foot in the door, allowing me to keep playing a part in the wonderful game. It will also keep me active. Fitness is important to me; I'd spend half my time in the gym whether I was a professional sportsman or not. I love the challenge of keeping myself fit and I can't ever imagine a time when I turn into a fat couch potato who gets out of breath brushing his teeth.

So, here I am, with one eye blinking and the other staring madly at my computer screen. I feel a little nervous about next season's move to Hull and fairly worried that my face will stay this way. But aside from those little issues, I have to say I've led a charmed existence. I have a beautiful wife, three smashing kids and mates for life. They're the three things that make me tick. Add my other passions – rugby, golf, tattoos and beer – and I've got the icing on the cake!

CHAPTER 17

A CROCK AND HULL STORY

If you've stuck with my daft ramblings this far you'll know I've had Saints blood running through my veins for most of my career. Well, I've now had a full transfusion and I'm 100 per cent Hull FC, the former foe at the other end of the M62. Of course, I still have a soft spot for everyone at Knowsley Road; I always will have. But I think I speak for every sportsman who's made a similar move when I say there's a glorious pleasure in turning your old team over. I reckon part of it is proving a point to them, and a big chunk is proving it to yourself, especially when you get to my age and you're not the devil-may-care lad you used to be. Then, for me, there are the Hull fans – as passionate and inspiring as any I've ever known. I'll talk more of those rugby-mad loons later.

I ended the first edition of this book with a face like a dropped pie. That was more than a year ago and I was serving my notice at my old club. My face is pretty much back to normal now (I say 'pretty' in its loosest sense) and I no longer scare my kids when I go to kiss them. The missus sometimes looks a bit wary, but only when my beard's particularly bushy!

It took a while to get over that nasty jaw injury but I was fit in time for the 2009 Grand Final, my last ever game for Saints. A win against Leeds that night would have been a fairytale ending to a dozen magical years so as I stepped out for the last time as the Saints' Number 7, I left nothing in the locker.

But it wasn't to be. It was a wet night and both teams worked hard and played well. It was a close game but Leeds played better and they won 18-10, making us runners-up for the third year in a row. It was the first season we'd finished empty-handed since 2003 and as the Leeds lads popped the champers and partied on the pitch with their trophy, I was gutted.

That night, we got the coach from Old Trafford back to the club and had a small party with all our wives and girlfriends. It was a tame affair, just a meal and a few glasses of wine. We'd lost so it was never going to be a wild one. As well as being the Grand Final bash, it was my leaving do and if we'd won, it would have been the party to end all parties; I'd have made sure of that. Though whether I'd still be here to tell the tale is a different matter.

The next day, I went on a pub crawl with the Saints lads and it ended up typically messy as we shared memories of our time together while drinking far too many pints. It inevitably spilled over into the following day – traditionally called Mad Monday – and about a dozen of us went out. We started in St Helens and went on to Liverpool. But I was showing my age and lack of drinking practise when I bailed out before midnight. Back in the day, I'd have been the last man staggering but I was first to order a taxi home from my own goodbye bash. Bloody hell, fetch me my slippers and a packet of Werther's Originals!

By Tuesday, the time to party and reminisce about Saints was over. I had a new and exciting chapter in my life to look forward to – as a Hull FC player. The Grand Final was on October 10 and I wasn't due at Hull until December. But I couldn't afford to sit around taking it easy so I was at my local gym every day keeping in shape. You don't turn up sloppy to a new club.

I was nervous as hell when I walked into their place at Brantingham for my first day's training. All the lads were having their breakfast and I got a few friendly nods and acknowledgements as I sat down. They were all taking the piss out of each other and cracking private jokes as I nervously supped my brew. It had been 12 years since I was the new boy at a club. Back then, I had the thickest skin on the planet and the cocky confidence of youth. Now, at the grand old age of 33, I was bricking it. It made me appreciate all the times a new player started at Saints and walked in to find us lot talking the kind of bollocks that only we understood. After all those years in my Saints comfort zone, it was really daunting.

I was minding my own business when Lee Radford, the captain, came over. I kind of knew Radders because he's been playing a long time, as long as me. We got chatting and he made me feel welcome. After a while I chilled out and realised as I surveyed the room that I wasn't the only new kid on the block. We'd made some big signings from Australia, like Mark O'Meley. He's more commonly known as Ogre – even his kids call him it! He's mad as fuck, much worse than me – and a top bloke. He's got the fun-loving attitude of a little kid, coupled with the ability to kill you with one finger before eating you whole. Then there's his fellow Aussie, Craig Fitzgibbon. Like Ogre, I hit it off with Fitzy straight away. Jordan Turner was another new face from a strange place where everyone talks funny. Oldham.

My first Hull training session was quite an experience. We did some weights in the morning and then some wrestling at Gordon Street, the legendary old stadium down at the boulevard. It was my first hand-in-ball practise for my new club and very nearly my last. They got us doing tackle tech, which means one player running at 50 per cent pace with the ball before another comes underneath and takes you to the ground (they've got padded mats). So there I was, running with the ball, when this young lad Liam Kent nailed me in the stomach with his shoulder, picked me up and dumped me on my fucking head. After a minute or two, I staggered to my feet while holding my neck and looking like I'd just aged about 40 years. The gaffer came over with a look on his face that said: 'Bloody hell, they warned me about taking on an old-timer and now he's been crocked by one of the kids.' He asked me if I was OK and I nodded. It would have been typical for me to break my neck before I'd even played a game and he must have been thinking the worst.

After that eye-watering experience, our pre-season training went well. It was tough but there weren't too many floggings, which is good for an old bloke like me. We did lots of ball work and I was calling the shots and we got to know each other pretty well. Once you're on the training field your rugby does the talking and you get to know your teammates that way. You soon become one of the boys.

In mid-December, we all went out for Christmas drinks at Bar Duice in Hull, which is co-owned by Radders. A few beers into the night, the gaffer took me to one side and asked me if I wanted to captain the side. I said I'd love to take it on as long as Radders was cool with it (he's a fucking tough bloke is Lee Radford and he can knock people out for fun). But Richard had already told him he was looking to change things around and he was cool with it. I was made up and we shook on it, but we had to keep it between ourselves for a few weeks until it was made official.

There was a big piece in the *Hull Daily Mail* a few days later, speculating about who would wear the Hull FC armband in 2010. The paper said it was between Radders, his vice-captain Peter Cusack, Fitzy and me. Richard formally announced my new role three weeks later while we were at pre-season training camp on the Vale of Glamorgan in Wales. I felt awkward, especially after knowing all about it for so long, but Radders was the first to come over and congratulate me. He was genuinely chuffed for me and he confirmed in my mind that I'd joined a team of great lads.

People have said they gave me the captaincy to calm me down, but that's bollocks. They just wanted to mix it up a bit. Radders is a forward and he doesn't spend 80 minutes on the field, whereas I'm on the field most of the time, organising the team and keeping everyone on their toes. It made sense to let me have a stab at it, especially with all my experience and the natural organisational role I play at scrum half. As I've mentioned earlier, I've never been too fussed about captaining a team. But I felt I was at the right time and place in my career to take the job on.

We were approaching the start of the 2010 season when I took a call off my old Saints mate Paul Wellens. 'Longy!' he said, 'I've just seen the fixture list and guess who we've got at the start of the season.' I knew straight away from the glee in his voice. I replied: 'It's us isn't it, bloody typical!' 'It gets better,' Wello said, 'It's at Knowsley Road!' Bloody hell, not only was I playing my old team in my first game for Hull, but it was at their place – the ground I used to call home.

In the weeks leading up to the game, returning to Knowsley Road was foremost in my mind. The press and the pundits were hyping it up with headlines like 'Prodigal son comes home'. Training went well and when the day came, I was trying to stay cool, like it was just any other game. But inside I was nervous as hell. I can honestly say it was the most nerve-racking lead up to any game of my life; worse than any Grand Final or Challenge Cup Final. I wondered what kind of reception I'd get off the Saints fans; would they boo me or would they cheer? It was the first time I'd been really bothered about the crowd's reaction. Even when I returned from the Bradford betting scandal ban and I was public enemy number one I didn't feel anything like this nervous.

The people of Hull are really passionate about their rugby; it's even more of a rugby league town than

Wigan or St Helens. Leading up to the Saints game, Hull FC fans were stopping me in the street to say they expected huge things in 2010. Hull FC were going places and they didn't want me, or any of the other big signings they'd made in the summer, letting them down. No pressure there, then!

When the day of the Saints game arrived, the team coach picked me up on the East Lancs Road just outside Wigan. It was weird as hell being on the away coach to Knowsley Road and as we drove through the gates, the nerves rushed through me. Luckily I'd already eaten my pre-match meal of baked spud, tuna, cheese and beans. I couldn't have managed a thing now, I was that nervous. But I hid my anxiety from my teammates. I'm the leader on the field so it was important I hid my nerves from the lads, especially the younger ones. It hardly instils confidence when the captain is shitting bricks.

I sat quietly in the dressing room, examining my tip sheet and chatting about strategy until I was called to toss the coin with the Saints captain. And God, was that a bizarre situation. There was me captaining Hull and stood opposite was my old Saints teammate, roommate and partner in crime Kez Cunningham. I won the toss and chose to kick off. Then, and I've never known this to happen between two rival captains, we gave each other a LOVE. It's usually a quick handshake and the odd word through gritted teeth or nothing. But there we were – HUGGING. It was like a scene from Brokeback Mountain!

Once the cuddling was over, I went to tell the lads we'd won the toss and took them out to warm up. When I got on the pitch, I got a few cheers off the Saints fans. I heard a few boos as well, but they were more like pantomime boos. It was foggy as hell out there on the pitch, a real pea-souper. We were told they were delaying the game for 15 minutes to see if it cleared up. It was no better when we came back out and we thought it was going to be called off. But, despite only being able to see 20 or 30 metres in front of us, they gave the all-clear to play.

Conditions-wise, it was pretty dreadful. Often when I kicked the ball, I had no idea where it ended up. It was even worse for the spectators. My brother was sat in the Saints end but he ended up with the Hull fans so he could see what was going on. Even the Sky cameras struggled to cover the game. It was like watching an old black and white portable telly in a bad reception area with a coat hanger for an aerial. The game was just about playable for us on the pitch, but it was crap for the fans, who could barely see a thing.

Despite the shocking conditions, it turned out to be a good game. Saints started on fire and for the first 20 minutes it was the fastest game I've ever played. They were legging it up the field like machines and I thought: 'So this is what it's like playing against St Helens. How good are these guys, how quick?' But we defended well and kept them from scoring.

Then we got a penalty right in front of the sticks after 20-odd minutes. Bero said: 'Let's go for goal' and I replied, 'No fucking chance, we're here now and we're going to try and stay here. They've had all the possession so far.' We played that set out and I got the ball, darted forward and hit Willie Manu and he gunned it straight through, crashed over and scored. We'd soaked up the pressure and hit them on the counter attack. The tide of the game had changed in our favour and I really felt it was ours for the taking. We went into the second half feeling comfortable and with Saints on the back foot. It was theirs to lose and ours to win.

In the second half Danny Tickle made a bust about 40 yards out from our try line, hit our full back Jordan Tansy who then hit Richard Horn. They were through and I thought, 'Fuck this, I'm going with them'. Horny drew the full back, passed it to me and I put my head down, ran the last 30 yards and scored. The Hull fans went mental and the lads all piled on me. My debut try for Hull was always going to be special but scoring it away at Saints was something else. It felt bloody wonderful but I was at the Saints end and I didn't want to rub it in by celebrating too much. So I walked off, feeling on top of the world and enjoying the roar of the Hull fans. When I got to our end I punched my fist into the air and shouted: 'Fucking come on!' My brother later told me that he's never been in a crowd like it.

Danny converted to take the score to 20-0, then a Tom Briscoe try and Fitzy conversion extended the lead and pretty much made the game ours. Matt Gidley scored a consolation try for the home side 10 minutes from time and my Saints replacement Kyle Eastmond added the touchline goal. But we had the final say when Kirk Yeaman latched onto my kick to end the game 32-12 and give me a dream start to my Hull career. I walked off the pitch feeling like my new club and me had done each other proud.

I couldn't have wished for a better debut but all in all it's been a stop-start season for me. A week after the

Saints game we were at home to Huddersfield and I pulled my hamstring early in the first half. I didn't want my new teammates and the fans thinking I was soft so I carried on. I was also conscious of the doubters who'd said Hull had made a mistake in signing an injury-prone bloke who's past his best. So I toughed it out when I should have come off and I ended up out of action for three weeks.

I came back from that injury in time for the Hull derby away at Craven Park on April 2. There's no town on this planet as rugby-mad as Hull and when FC and KR come together it's a massive occasion. The atmosphere was crazy. More than 10,000 fans packed the stadium that Good Friday and our supporters were outnumbered by about four to one. But you wouldn't know it from the noise coming from our end.

So much is at stake at a derby, especially when the rivalry's as bitter as it is on Humberside. A win gives your fans bragging rights for weeks, be it down the pub, at work, at school or in the day room at the old folks' home. The sense of occasion and the desire to win makes it different from other league games. You can throw the formbook out the window on derby day.

It was a typically tough and hard-fought game and we won 18-14 after some heroic defending. It was only our second win in eight attempts against our neighbours and a great bonus for our gaffer Richard, who'd just signed a new two-year deal with the club.

Speaking of Hull KR, I'd like to take this opportunity to thank them for the lovely nickname they chant at me from the terraces: 'Rent Boy'. Wigan fans sing 'Sean Long is a wanker', an accusation I won't try to deny. Similarly,

I can't really defend myself against those wits at Leeds who sing, 'Where's your caravan' to the tune of the 1971 hit 'Chirpy, Chirpy, Cheep, Cheep'. Of course, when Leeds fans aren't in a musical mood, they prefer to get straight to the point with: 'Gypo, Gypo, Gypo!' Yes, I lived in a mobile home back in the day and if that makes me a gypsy, then fair enough. But 'rent boy'? Even when times were hard, my arse was never for sale.

Anyway, we got the derby win and the Hull FC camp was a happy one. But I wasn't buzzing for long because three days later, on Easter Monday, I bust my ankle ligaments against Warrington. It could have happened to anyone and it was just bad luck. I was out then for five games.

I was back in time for our second league tie against Saints at the KC on June 4. It was one of the most exciting and dramatic games I've ever played in, featuring a comeback that ranks up there with the 'Wide to West' classic. But I came very close to missing it.

The day before the game I was really ill with a vomiting and diarrhoea bug (the good old Longy luck strikes again!). I will spare you the gory details, but it's safe to say I was curled in a ball projecting unspeakable stuff from both ends. I was on my own at my place in Hull and I spent the night dividing my time between sitting on and kneeling over the toilet. The following morning – match day – woke up on the bathroom floor with my pants round my ankles and my face stuck to the carpet with vomit. You'd think I'd been out for a 'swift half' with Johnny Vegas!

I staggered to the sink and tried a drink of water but it came straight back up. I was due to play in a few hours so I texted the physio who advised me to get straight to A&E. The docs examined me and said I was really dehydrated and they put me on a drip for a few hours and pumped six litres of fluid into me. I felt better afterwards, though far from 100 per cent, and they let me go home.

To be honest, if it had been any other game I'd have fucked it off. But I'd need to be at Death's door to miss my second game against Saints. No way was I denying myself the chance to make it two out of two against my old club. Plus, we'd trained well all week and I was key to the tactics we'd been practising; I didn't want to let the boys down.

As we ran on the pitch that night I felt fine. I knew I should have felt awful after bugger-all sleep and a nasty bug, but the sense of occasion and the adrenaline sorted me out. There was plenty of time to crash and recover once the game was over.

Clearly out to get revenge for their opening round defeat, Saints were on fire in the first half. Francis 'Franny' Meli was back from a hamstring injury and played out of his skin, grabbing four tries in the opening 44 minutes. We were 20 points down early in the second half and looked on course for a thrashing.

Saints were really quick, aggressive and confident while we couldn't get hold of the ball and kept giving penalties away. Their 20-point lead could easily have been 50 but all of a sudden we reversed it. We upped the speed of the ruck and Saints couldn't keep up with us. We did to them what they'd been doing to us and our forwards got us on the front foot. We were on a roll and the tables were turning.

We scored a try and I thought, 'We're back in it here'. We built a bit of pressure and we scored again and the crowd was going wild, really getting behind us. Saints suffered a blow when my old pal James Roby had to leave the pitch in a daze and that's when we really took charge. I lofted a kick and it bounced nicely to Danny Houghton for an easy try. Everything was going our way. We'd snatched the momentum and, with Saints on the back foot, Willie Manu took advantage of a penalty on their line to barge over and cut the deficit to four points. Then, in the dying minutes, I put up a kick to my old mate Franny's wing (he might be able to score four tries but I know he's capable of the odd error) and it paid off when Danny Tickle scrambled the ball over the top to draw us level.

At 26 apiece I knew there was only going to be one winner and we played with confidence. I had a couple of shots at drop goal, one of them dropping just in front of the cross bar, and the other that was, well, fucking shit. Then in the last minute of the game, we had possession about 30 metres out and Danny did what I hadn't managed to do and slotted home a one pointer to win the game. The crowd were delirious and so were we. It was a cracking game, both to play in and to watch.

It's very rare for any team to do the double over Saints. To come back from 20 points down in the second half is fantastic. I spoke to Kez after the game and he said to me: 'How good do you feel now?' I replied: 'Sweet mate, fucking sweet.'

Since I moved to Hull I'm often asked how we compare to Saints. Basically, I reckon the players we've got are on a par with them in terms of ability. But what Saints have that we lack is the self-belief and the confidence that comes with being a high-achieving top-flight club for well over a decade. They have young lads coming through like Kyle Eastmond, Andrew Dixon, Jonny Lomax and Gary Wheeler who've been brought up with top players and success all around them. It's a great confidence-builder.

At Hull, the lads have a great work ethic and they go the extra mile in training, more so than we did when I was at Saints. But our form is inconsistent and it's largely down to confidence. We've been unlucky injury-wise this season, with me, Fitzy, Willie Manu and Shaun Berrigan all missing several games. Obviously when key players are crocked, it's crucial that the lads who come in to replace them can do the job. They do it at Saints but I think some of our lads need to believe they can go out there and do it because they are just as good as the Saints players.

As I write this, my left arm's in a sling. My typing's not great at the best of times, but doing it with one hand is a bloody nightmare. Last Friday (June 25) I dislocated my right elbow in a bone-crunching clash with the 17 stone of pure muscle that is my teammate Willie Manu. We won 10-8 and the scoreline reflects the rather forgettable match it was. But it will be etched on my mind for many years as the game that ruled me out for the crucial end of season run.

It was a freak accident that could have happened to anyone. I kicked the ball deep into the Catalans corner, turning their winger Dane Carlaw. I was leading the chase and as Dane got close to me, he stepped to my left.

I went to hit him with my left shoulder and wrap him up then BANG – Manu hit him and my arm at the same time. My elbow popped out of its socket and the pain was excruciating - it made my todger piercing seem like a paper cut!

I hit the floor in agony and within seconds the doc was over me, asking if I was okay. With words too colourful to repeat here, I said I needed someone to stick my elbow back in. He tried but it had gone into spasm and there was nothing he could do. They gave me some gas and air, which did bugger all. Ask any woman who's given birth and she'll tell you gas and air makes precious little difference at the peak of pain. It's about as useful as a sticking plaster on a severed head.

I was rushed by ambulance to Hull Royal Infirmary where they sorted my pain out with a nice hit of morphine. Later that night (I don't remember much) they knocked me out and put my arm back in the socket. I woke up the next day in pain, but at least my arm was no longer pointing in two directions. A few days later I saw a specialist in Wrexham who, thankfully, said I didn't need an operation. He ruled me out of playing action for eight to ten weeks, which was a massive blow, but thankfully I'd be back in time for the play-offs. An operation would have set me back at least a month more. As I write this, we are fourth in the table and I hope that the boys would continue to do the business until I got back.

Before this latest setback, I'd missed seven games this season because of hamstring and ankle problems. If you add the time I'm likely to be out of action with my arm, I've been fit for an average of about one game in two. Naturally, it's a crushing statistic for me because the more games you play the better you feel. But we've only lost two games when I've played so I'm beginning to show the fans what I can do and why I was signed. It would be nice to have had an injury-free season but it could be a lot worse. I have no long-term injury complaints and when I'm not crocked, I feel as fit as I've ever been. My pace hasn't gone; I intercepted against Castleford the other day and legged it 70 metres. I admit to being a little bit slower as I approach my 34th birthday in September but I've finished off a few 40-metre tries this season without being caught.

Of course, some of the media people are saying this latest injury spells the end of my career. Well, they know where they can shove their opinions. I will come back better than ever, like I always do when the chips are down. If the reporters and pundits want to write me off, then let them do it. They've been having a go all my career and I prove them wrong every time. To be honest, if I was playing badly when I dislocated my elbow I would be worried about coming back. But I have been on the top of my game and really enjoying it.

I hope to keep playing for a while yet. I'm contracted to Hull till the end of next season and if they want to keep me on after that, I'm happy to stay. As I've said earlier, when I finally hang up my boots I plan to coach. The younger lads at Hull are always coming to me for advice and I love passing my knowledge on to anyone who wants it. I passed my coaching exams in April so I'm now qualified to coach any Super League team. It means that if the worst happened and my career ended with a horror injury, I could get straight into coaching. It's something I reckon I could do well.

A CROCK AND HULL STORY

In the time I've been injured this season, I've not been sat at home twiddling my thumbs. I sit with the gaffer watching videos of the team and we talk tactics. I would happily talk rugby all day and it doesn't feel like work to me. During games, I sit with Richard in the stand and tell him what I'd be saying to the lads if I were playing. Obviously, I leave shouting out the orders to him!

As well as getting involved in the coaching side, I've been broadening my horizons with a bit of radio work. I've commentated on two games for BBC Radio Five Live and one for KFC Live and I really enjoy it. But let's face it, being paid to watch a game of rugby and talk about it is a no brainer for me. It's what I'd be doing with my mates anyway. The only difference is I have a microphone in front of me and I can't swear! In an ideal world, I'll coach for a decade or two then get into media work.

Speaking of the media, a newspaper asked me recently how I felt about England's chances in the upcoming Four Nations tournament. I declined to comment because I wanted to express my thoughts here as I feel quite strongly about the subject.

Basically, I reckon our forwards are better than the Aussies and the Kiwis. And we've got two great half backs in Sam Tomkins and Kyle Eastmond, the young stars of the Super League. They've both been outstanding this year and they're going to get better, although Kyle has had his share of injuries which could keep him out of the Four Nations. The England team will really benefit from having those two. If they work hard on their game and keep improving (which they are) they'll be up there with the best in the world.

The problem we have on the international stage is our three quarters who really bring the England squad down. Don't get me wrong, they're all decent players. But Aussie greats like Greg Inglis and Israel Folau blow them away. If anything, it's our pack that will do it for us. In recent history, they've kept our head above water in the international game. Players such as Adrian Morley and Jamie Peacock and new lads like Sam Burgess and Gareth Ellis (who play in Australia), and my ex-Saints teammates James Roby and James 'Jammer' Graham – they make up a really good pack. For years we've been able to win one-off tests because our pack drags us through. This year is no different. But I really can't see them pulling it off for three consecutive games.

I blame much of the state of our international game on the number of Aussies who come over here to play in the Super League. There are quality players like my Hull pals Fitzy, Ogre and Manu who bring a lot to our domestic game. Fitzy, for instance, is a legend, a real tough competitor. He's played for New South Wales and for his country and he's a welcome addition to our game. Guys like him that ooze class, I don't mind.

What I don't like is when shit players can't make it Down Under who come over here and take the places of our home-grown talent. We should be pushing our British youngsters through. Managers are willing to pay these guys more money because it's the easier option. They want a quick fix. It's easy for them to take someone on with playing experience and match confidence than give a new lad a shot. You need to give young players a year or two to find their feet. They have to make a few mistakes and develop. It was a bit like that for me at

Wigan; they wanted a quick fix and I wasn't ready so they fucked me off in favour of more experienced players, regardless of my future potential.

We have home grown star players like Eastmond and Tomkins who've come though and if it wasn't for all the ordinary journeymen Aussies that come here, there would be scope for more kids like them to flourish too. If we looked after our young talent better and gave them the opportunities and the investment, we would not be going into the Four Nations as the underdogs we are. We have a lot of poor Aussies playing in three quarter positions for our domestic teams and our national squad suffers as a result.

Of course, it's a big ask for us to ever overtake the Aussies to be the best in the world. Rugby league is the main sport there so they have a massive pool of players to pick from. I really can't see us ever being as consistently strong as Australia for that reason. And as I mentioned in an earlier chapter of this book, I don't think it helps that our season is so much longer. We play more games throughout the season followed by the Challenge Cup competition so it's bound to take it out of you by the end of the year. Our national squad does not have enough preparation. It's thrown together and expected to gel over a couple of weeks.

Last time we played in the Tri nations in 2006, we went out to Australia and New Zealand late. The powers that be are trying to change it now because they know we need more preparation and more time together as a team. So if they do that and we play the same amount of games as Australia, we are on a level playing field. We have no excuses then. If we do that and we look after our domestic talent, we stand a chance of being an all round solid team in a few years.

Right, rant over. But before I go, I'd like to share a tale that pretty much sums up the passion of the Airlie Bird faithful. We played the Catalans at their place on May 15 and we won 28-14. It was a tough game and we were all away from home, so the gaffer treated us to a night out near to where we were staying in Perpignan. He stuck a few hundred Euros behind the bar and I was stood with the lads, sampling the local lager, when this woman came up to be with a face like thunder. She was in her forties and wearing a Hull FC top – there were a few fans in the pub – and she said: 'What the Hell do you think you are playing at?'

I was only on my second pint so I was sure I hadn't yet stripped naked or taken a dump on a table, so I glanced behind me, thinking she was talking to someone else. But then she prodded my chest and asked: 'Well?' A few of the lads had gathered round by this point and I said: 'Nothing, what's up?' She then looked up and demanded: 'What the bloody hell's that on your head?' Feeling a bit nervous at how this exchange was going, I looked to my teammates for back-up in case things turned nasty and replied: 'It's a bandana.' Her face got angrier and she snapped: 'It's red and bloody white! Hull KR are red and bloody white! We're BLACK and white. Now get it off – now!'

I didn't need telling twice and it was off my head in a flash. I apologised for being so stupid and explained that I'd really not given it any thought. Even though I played for Hull FC, I – and all my teammates for that matter – didn't realise that I was sporting a headband in our arch-rivals' colours. In hindsight, it was a shocking oversight and it went to show that it's the fans that really carry the torch for this great sport of ours.

The lady who gave me a dressing down that night had probably been supporting Hull FC since before I even picked up a ball. It's die-hard fans like her who spend their hard-earned cash travelling the globe in all weathers to will us on at every game. When you've played a shocker and you're praying for the whistle in the dying minutes, it's people like her who'll shout encouragement from the terraces to keep you going. And I've got nothing but respect and appreciation for them.

After that incident I vowed to stay clear of anything red and white. I just hope my kids don't ask me to dress up as Santa this Christmas!